SINGAPORE
PERSPECTIVES
2010
Home.Heart.Horizon.

SINGAPORE
PERSPECTIVES
2010
Home.Heart.Horizon.

Edited by
Tan Tarn How

LKY Lee Kuan Yew
School of Public Policy
National University of Singapore

iPS Institute of
Policy Studies

World Scientific

Published by

World Scientific Publishing Co. Pte. Ltd.

5 Toh Tuck Link, Singapore 596224

USA office: 27 Warren Street, Suite 401-402, Hackensack, NJ 07601

UK office: 57 Shelton Street, Covent Garden, London WC2H 9HE

British Library Cataloguing-in-Publication Data
A catalogue record for this book is available from the British Library.

SINGAPORE PERSPECTIVES 2010: Home.Heart.Horizon.

Copyright © 2010 by World Scientific Publishing Co. Pte. Ltd.

ISBN-13 978-981-4322-41-6 (pbk)
ISBN-10 981-4322-41-5 (pbk)

Printed by FuIsland Offset Printing (S) Pte Ltd. Singapore

Contents

Foreword

When the theme for Singapore Perspectives 2010 was first conceptualised, a review of the achievement of the various aspirations in the National Pledge was initially identified as a possibility. However, after the National Day Parade in 2009, it was decided that the Singapore Perspectives 2010 should go further and examine the meaning of Singapore as a home, its future prospects, and how Singaporeans feel for the country and for their fellow Singaporeans.

Occupying a very unique position in the global milieu, Singapore has to develop novel solutions to manage its ever changing challenges. Its city-state status, its open multi-ethnic society and the degree to which it is connected to the world cannot be taken for granted. In order to ensure the applicability and suitability of new ideas, local factors need to be taken into consideration alongside global trends.

Through the prisms of "Home", "Heart" and "Horizon", the three panels of the Singapore Perspectives 2010 Conference, "One United People", "One Gracious Society" and "One Global City", addressed issues imperative to Singapore's continued growth and success. With the term "Home" referring to the fundamental elements that make Singapore "tick" in an era of greater mobility across the globe, "Heart" referring to compassion and openness amongst Singaporeans, and "Horizon" evoking the possibilities of the future for the city-state, the speakers drew out views and ideas from a wide spectrum of society, provoking thoughts and engaging audience participation. An active exchange and reflection from a varied background is necessary in the creation of a better tomorrow and in enriching Singaporeans' understanding of the dynamics which characterise our society. This process strengthens the openness of one's mind and clarity of thought, and maintains the balance of individual perspectives and community attitudes, a fundamental ingredient in sustaining Singapore's development.

Singapore Perspectives is the flagship event of the Institute of Policy Studies. Through the years, it has achieved a good standing and has a good following as the Conference systematically addresses issues of significance to Singapore's society and its future. Encouraging different perspectives to be raised and examined, the annual Singapore Perspectives Conference is an ideal platform for individuals to come together and mull over the myriad of challenges Singapore faces and the solutions needed.

Going forward, there is a need to enlarge Singaporeans' mind share on how to preserve what we have, improve on the ways we govern ourselves, and secure the unique Singapore we call home. We hope the contents of this book will provide insight for further discussion and strengthen the passion and "can-do" spirit amongst Singaporeans.

Team SP2010:
Tan Simin, Chua Chun Ser, Stephanie Neubronner, Debbie Soon
and
Ong Keng Yong

Acknowledgements

The Institute of Policy Studies is grateful to the following institutions for their support of Singapore Perspectives 2010 held on Monday, 25 January 2010.

Made possible by

Képpel Corporation

Standard Chartered

TEMASEK HOLDINGS

Supported by

HILL & KNOWLTON

HOUSING & DEVELOPMENT BOARD

ITE
Institute of Technical Education

Jardine Cycle & Carriage

KPMG

M P A
SINGAPORE

NYP Nanyang Polytechnic

NANYANG TECHNOLOGICAL UNIVERSITY

NUS
National University of Singapore

NGEE ANN
POLYTECHNIC

Supported by

PHILIPS

REPUBLIC
POLYTECHNIC

SIM
UNIVERSITY

SMU
SINGAPORE MANAGEMENT
UNIVERSITY
10TH ANNIVERSARY | 2000-2010

SINGAPORE
POLYTECHNIC

SMRT

ST ®

TEMASEK
POLYTECHNIC

Editor's
Acknowledgements

We worked under a tight deadline to get this book out as soon as possible, and in this light I would like to thank all the authors for being so understanding. Without exception they turned in their papers on time, two weeks after the conference, and responded promptly to every request for information and clarification. One even spent part of her holiday finishing her manuscript, an act which we met with equal measures of gratitude and guilt.

From IPS, I would like to thank Chua Chun Ser and Stephanie Neubronner for helping with the preparation of parts of the manuscript, and to Gillian Koh and Catherine Lim for the coordinating the publication of the book. Most of all, my heartfelt thanks to Tan Simin who did a magnificent job of managing the project, offered many excellent ideas on improving the manuscript and gave a careful reading of the texts — all under great time pressure.

Tan Tarn How

Home.Heart.Horizon

Conference Concept

Singapore's position in the global milieu is unique. Its city-state status, its open multi-ethnic society and the degree to which it is connected to the world mean that novel solutions to manage its challenges have to be developed. Very often, local factors have to be taken into consideration in tandem with global trends.

Singapore Perspectives 2010: Home.Heart.Horizon. seeks to examine the myriad of challenges and solutions which Singapore faces today through the prisms of "Home", "Heart" and "Horizon". The term "Home" refers to the fundamentals that make Singapore "tick" in an era of greater mobility across the globe. What more needs to be done to maintain Singapore's success? "Heart" refers to compassion and openness amongst Singaporeans. It embodies soul, conscience and considerateness. Are Singaporeans compassionate, rooted with a strong sense of belonging, commitment and desire to contribute to society's well-being? Finally, the term "Horizon" evokes the possibilities of the future for the city-state. Singapore must continue to "scan the horizon" to remain outward-looking in order to maintain its relevance in today's world by developing capabilities to spot both looming challenges and opportunities.

Singapore Perspectives 2010 will address the elements of "Home", "Heart" and "Horizon" in three panels — One United People, One Gracious Society and One Global City — within the context of Singapore's unique position.

Welcome Remarks

ONG KENG YONG
Tuesday 26 January 2010
Raffles City Convention Centre

Prime Minister Lee Hsien Loong, distinguished guests, friends, ladies and gentlemen:

1   A very good morning to you. I am pleased to welcome you to the 11th edition of Singapore Perspectives. This is the Institute's flagship conference. It began in the year 2000. Before that, the Institute had organised a series called "Year in Review".

2   Over the years, we have had several Cabinet Ministers attend and speak at Singapore Perspectives, including Minister Mentor Lee Kuan Yew in 2008. However, this is the first time the Prime Minister is speaking at Singapore Perspectives. Thank you, Mr Lee, for spending time with us this morning.

3   Today, we have an impressive line-up of speakers who will discuss and debate the issues associated with the conference's theme of "Home.Heart.Horizon."

4   To give you a bit of background: when we first started conceptualising the theme for this year's conference, we actually wanted to examine the achievement of the various aspirations outlined in the National Pledge. After the National Day Parade in 2009, however, we decided to go further and look at the meaning of Singapore as a home, our heartfelt feelings for Singapore and fellow Singaporeans, as well as the country's prospects going

into the future. This resulted in the three panels we have in the conference, namely, "One United People", "One Gracious Society" and "One Global City".

5   I understand from the speakers that they intend to offer their respective perspectives to provoke your thoughts and engage your participation. The seating arrangement today has been designed to facilitate interaction amongst conference participants. Do feel free to comment and ask questions of our speakers and of each other so as to make it an even more worthwhile day for yourself.

6   Our speakers today come from a wide variety of backgrounds, representing the multi-faceted nature of Singapore society. This is what Singapore Perspectives is about: to draw in views and ideas from as wide a spectrum of society as possible.

7   We hope you will find today's programme rewarding. More importantly, we hope that you will leave today feeling challenged and inspired.

8   As you can see on this backdrop, we have also received strong support from institutions of higher learning, statutory boards and outstanding companies from the private sector. Singapore Perspectives would not be possible without their kind and continuous support. I would like to make a special mention of Keppel Corporation, Standard Chartered and Temasek Holdings, which have made many IPS events possible. IPS looks forward to many more years of cooperation with all the sponsors.

9   Let me also take this opportunity to thank you for being with us today.

10   I would now like to invite the Prime Minister, Mr Lee Hsien Loong, to deliver his Keynote Address. Mr Lee, please.

Keynote Address

PRIME MINISTER LEE HSIEN LOONG

Mr Ong Keng Yong, Director of the Institute of Policy Studies, distinguished guests, ladies and gentlemen.

I am very happy to join you this morning for the 11th edition of the Singapore Perspectives 2010.

Singapore has just gone through two very difficult years. The problems became acute in 2008 when the US and European financial systems nearly collapsed, dragging down real economies worldwide. We were also dragged down faster than others because we are more open and globalised, and by January 2009, our economy was facing a drastic plunge. Therefore, over the last one year, we have focused on dealing with the downturn, working with employers and unions to save jobs, supporting viable companies with needed financing, and helping Singaporeans to pull through the crisis. The year turned out much better than we had feared. This was partly because globally the worst scenarios which we had imagined fortunately did not materialise, and also because the measures we took — the Resilience Package — were effective and helped to keep companies afloat, workers in jobs and to keep confidence up and morale high. Now we are moving ahead again with cautious confidence.

Even while we tackle the crisis, we kept our eyes on the long term and took steps to prepare for our future. We acted to restructure the economy, to address our population shortfalls, and to update our political system. These are not one-off projects, but major continuing priorities and we will continue to work on them this year and for some time to come. In some cases, I think, for a long time to come.

First, we need to restructure our economy to maximise our growth, our potential and what we are able to deliver. We need to do this to respond to the changed external environment and also to adapt to our domestic physical limits. The global crisis has made this a more urgent task. Worldwide, growth will remain weak for several years to come. The US consumers, in particular, will be less free spending. Therefore, we will have to work harder to expand our markets in the developed countries. In Asia, economies are continuing to transform themselves, not just China and India, but in ASEAN too. Countries like Vietnam, which I visited last week, are moving ahead strongly.

This creates a window of opportunity for us because we are ahead of the other Asian countries. We can service them, help them to make the transformation and development and growth and, in the process, move ahead and benefit our economy and transform ourselves. But Asia's rise also means growing competition because as the other countries enhance their capabilities, they will narrow the gap with the developed countries and increasingly be able to do what we have been doing.

Domestically, we face increasing constraints, especially in land and labour. Our total land area is finite and very little is lying fallow. Our own population is only growing slowly and we cannot indefinitely expand our workforce by importing more and more foreign workers from abroad. Hence, we have to adjust our growth strategy and find new ways to continue to do well. We have to shift to growing qualitatively, not just by expansion but by upgrading. We have to extract maximum value from the resources that we have. Every piece of land must be put to optimum use. Activities which are no longer competitive or productive have to be phased out gradually and replaced by activities which are more productive and competitive. We have to upgrade our workers, both our own as well as the foreign workers who are here, and enhance the quality of our workforce and what we are able to deliver individually and as a team.

Taking it in terms of overall macro numbers, we will have to improve our productivity performance sharply, as Senior Minister Goh Chok Tong noted yesterday. Over the last decade or so, productivity growth has averaged only 1% a year. We have to double this and improve it to 2 to 3% per year and this will take a major effort. But we have to do it so that progressively and inexorably our economy will be transformed. Then, provided we can raise our productivity, even if our total GDP grows more slowly, our workers can become more productive and our income per capita can continue to rise. Becoming more productive is not just a matter of working harder but also means restructuring, change and flux; uncertainties, experiments and discontinuities. Businesses need to innovate relentlessly, phasing out unproductive activities and shifting into more fruitful areas. They have to be bold and seek out opportunities in distant shores. They have to be ready for fresh competition — new players able to do better and always threatening to steal their cheese. Workers cannot expect to be carried along by a generally rising tide. They too have to be psychologically prepared to adapt, to change and to make the effort to upgrade themselves, not just once but continually throughout their working lives.

Singapore can and must continue to do better year by year to take advantage of the abundant opportunities in Asia. Our standing is high, our capabilities are growing. People want to do business in Singapore and look towards Singapore for ideas, for models and for opportunities to link up and cooperate. We must take full advantage of this strong position. But overall, we must acknowledge that we are now more developed economically than we were 10 or 15 years ago and we can no longer grow as rapidly as before. Over the last decade, from 1999 to 2009, our growth averaged 5% per year, which is a remarkable achievement considering the level at which we already were 10 years ago. Looking ahead, there are two balancing factors. One, we aim to have higher productivity growth but two, realistically our workforce will expand more slowly. If we take these two factors together, I think it will be very difficult for us to average 5% growth over the next 10 years. There will be good years when we should go faster and there will be other years which are tough, when we will do more poorly. But overall, if you take it over the next decade, I think 5% will be a stretch. So the Ministry of Trade & Industry is now studying what the realistic long-term growth target will be. Our economic strategies and policies have to facilitate this transition to enable the economy to perform to its limits and help Singaporeans to thrive in the new world. The Economic Strategies Committee chaired by the Finance Minister Tharman Shanmugaratnam will publish its recommendations next week and the government will respond in the Budget three weeks after that.

One key to sustaining economic growth is to rejuvenate our population and to develop and attract talent. The best economic policy will not bring us growth if our population starts to decline or if we are denuded of talent and lacked the ability and drive to solve problems, create opportunities or lead Singapore, whether it is in government, in business or in society.

Unfortunately, our birth rates despite our best efforts are not improving. Last year, there were fewer births than in 2008 despite all the measures we implemented back in 2008. Our statisticians tell me there were 170 fewer births. It may not seem to be a lot less but it is a lot less than it ought to be in terms of total numbers and it means that our Total Fertility Rate would have gone down further. Maybe it was because of the economic troubles but even then, this is a grave trend which if unchecked will cause us to have a shrinking population, and not just a rapidly ageing population. We have to encourage Singaporeans to start families through parenthood benefits and change in attitudes, and other incentives and social adjustments. But we must also top up our population and talent pool with immigrants in a measured and calibrated way. Immigration has become a more sensitive issue for Singaporeans. It is a policy which is ultimately designed to benefit Singaporeans but some citizens perceive newcomers as unwelcome extra competition for jobs, for school places, for housing. The Government understands these sentiments. We are distinguishing more clearly between and permanent residents in subsidies, in healthcare and school places sectors. We are also moderating the inflow so that it is not too fast for us to absorb. We do not want to shift the tenor of our society, we do not want to dilute the Singapore spirit and we must not make Singaporeans feel that our home has become different or alien. These adjustments should take the edge off the unhappiness and make it easier for citizens to accept the inflow but immigration is going to be an issue which will be with us for some time because we have no alternative to topping up our population numbers. Therefore, we have to examine dispassionately, understand the realities, the forces, the imperatives we face and manage the issue and our programmes pragmatically.

We also have to work at integration. New citizens have to make the effort to adjust to our social norms and Singaporeans too must open their hearts and accommodate the new arrivals. Then, gradually we can become one people, just as our forefathers had started out as immigrants from different lands and gradually unite as fellow citizens. While dealing with new stresses, we must not forget our society's old fault lines. Our various races and religions enjoy good relations here in Singapore but it is only the result of constant tending and vigilance. Race and religion remain very sensitive issues in Southeast Asia. You just look at the current tensions in Malaysia over the use of the word 'Allah' by non-Muslims and the attacks on churches and *suraus* over the last few months. We must not let our guard down or allow these external problems to affect our own precious and unique harmony in Singapore.

Underpinning our ability to tackle all these challenges, whether it is economic, demographic or any other challenges, is a good political system — a system which will ensure a stable and capable government, good leadership and an engaged electorate.

Our political system cannot be static or frozen but must evolve with the times. We are making significant changes to the election system. We will have more Non-Constituency MPs, more Single Member Constituencies, smaller Group Representation Constituencies and we are going to affirm the Nominated MP system, so that it will automatically happen and be part of our Parliament. We are also introducing a "cooling-off" day on the eve of polling day at the end of each election campaign. These changes will ensure a more diverse set of voices in Parliament and enable us to reflect in our political system a wider range of views in society. It will encourage Singaporeans to engage in national issues. I hope they will foster rational debate, wise collective decisions and enable the government to act decisively once a consensus is reached. A weak government or divisive national politics would be disastrous for Singapore. We are making these changes in good time. There is a mini general election fever in town. The general election is due sometime within the next two years. But it is not imminent. We are putting the legislation in place now so that everything will be ready when the elections are called.

Having a sound political system is essential but in itself it is not enough to produce political stability or good government. That still depends on having the right people in-charge — an able, committed team coming forward to lead the country and take responsibility for our future. Therefore, a key task for my predecessors and me has always been to identify promising people to form the next team. We have been making

9

good progress on this. We do not have a complete team lined up in the Cabinet or in government yet, but I am confident that by the next general election, the PAP (Peoples' Action Party) will field a team which will contain the core of the next generation leadership who can, in time, take over from me and my present colleagues and assure the country's future for the next 10 to 20 years. And this leadership renewal will be a major issue in the next general election. Finding the next team who can make sure that Singapore can endure and can give investors as well as Singaporeans the confidence that what is here will be here a generation from now after the present faces have faded from the scene is the most important issue in the next general election, whenever that will be.

So we have to make fundamental adjustments in these three areas — in our economic policies, in our demographics and in our political system. We will move carefully, each time taking small steps but cumulatively making major changes. We will take a progressive approach but despite this, change will be unsettling for Singaporeans. Economic change means greater risk of people losing jobs and having to retrain for new jobs. Demographic change means difficulties of accommodating new immigrants. Political changes pose challenges of maintaining cohesion and unity while airing more diverse views and interests. Navigating these problems is not just a matter of getting the policies right but of communication and persuasion, being sensitive to Singaporeans' concerns and yet not losing the bigger picture. In other words, the human aspects of leadership in government. We have to bring people along to understand what is happening and why we have to reach a consensus on the way forward. We have to strengthen our bonds with each challenge that we meet and tackle together.

It is critical for us to have regular, continual conversations on these issues — airing different views, discussing and analysing problems, examining alternative approaches and solutions. The Institute of Policy Studies provides such a forum for this purpose. That is why it was created in the first place. The Institute organises public discussions on issues of the day. It aims to encourage a critical group, the intelligentsia — people who follow policies, who have an interest, and we hope, have informed views about matters. Informed debate among opinion leaders provides the essential backdrop to policy-making. The Government does not work in a vacuum. It works in a context of a society, of a tone in the society, of opinions, of views; what do people feel, what do they consider to be possible to do and beyond that possibility, what can the government help them to achieve, not just what they imagine they can do but something more; something beyond the expectations, but yet it is something which is realistic and which we can do together.

Informed debate, therefore, sets a tone of the national discourse, helps to shape the broad understanding of issues among the population and thus enables the society to consider more options and to make more informed choices. The IPS is independent of the government, but it is useful for the public sector to cooperate with the IPS and to be forthcoming with information and access, for example, when IPS holds public forums or conducts policy research. This way, the government can consult more widely and develop better thought-out policies, and IPS will be more effective in fostering informed discussion of policies outside government. I know there are quite a number of people from various government departments who are attending this session today. So I am putting in this little plug on behalf of IPS. I hope they will take note.

Today's conference theme "Home.Heart.Horizon." is directly relevant to the economic, population and political issues which I discussed.

Start with Horizon. Whatever the difficulties of globalisation, we have got to connect ourselves to the world and reach out to the distant horizon, and in fact, all over the world. We must do this in order to make a living for ourselves, let alone to prosper. But we also must do this in order to attract talent and to develop our own talent by exposing them to the wide world.

Heart: We have to feel that we are one people, that despite differences in race, language and religion and whether we are new or old citizens, we are Singaporeans together. We compete against one another but we must also empathise with and support each other, especially our less fortunate compatriots. We can do this through philanthropy, volunteerism, corporate social responsibility and daily acts of kindness. When a project like Ren Ci Community Hospital raises funds and puts on a charity show, which they did last night, they were able to raise $7 million from Singaporeans, through donations and phone-ins, big and small. That is a sign that we care, that we are prepared to chip in and we will work together not just to make this a better place but to make this a humane, warm place where we feel we are Singaporeans together as one big family. We have to understand that we

11

are in this together and despite whatever differences we may have, we will push forward in the same direction. Therefore, economic policy is not just a matter of attaining the highest possible GDP growth number but also ensuring the quality of growth and enabling all Singaporeans to benefit from the country's progress. Population policy is also not just a matter of numbers, having the right total size of the population but also of managing the social impact of the inflows and building bonds between different groups of Singaporeans.

We must make this our home. Singaporeans must feel that they are part of this nation's progress, that we belong here, that we all have a stake in Singapore, and that our future is here. Then we will commit ourselves to Singapore and work together to make it even better for our children's generation. This idea of home applies even to overseas Singaporeans. There are more than 180,000 who work, study or live overseas at any time. We hope that wherever you are, whatever you are doing, Singapore will forever be in your hearts and you will always remember that Singapore is here waiting for you.

I have always followed carefully the reports of IPS' flagship annual conference. I do not always agree with the views expressed. I should say I do not always disagree with the criticisms made. But I have always found the discussions valuable because they give a sense of how informed observers, especially those outside the government, view government policies and economic, social and political developments in Singapore and around us. I am confident that this conference will be equally fruitful and successful. I hope IPS will continue to do this over the years and in this way, help Singapore to make the right choices and build better lives for all. Thank you very much.

One United People

This panel examines Singapore's development and nation-building in relation to social cohesion. Recent public discussions on the national pledge and the increasing number of immigrants and new Singaporeans have raised questions about the strength of our social fabric. Within a changing social landscape, more interest groups are emerging. It is timely to critically assess the policies and practices that aim to deliver the ideal of "one united people". Can Singaporeans maintain civilities and let different viewpoints and practices flourish? Some Singaporeans are inclined towards a different approach. How can we balance the aspirations of Singaporeans in an increasingly differentiated "Home"?

CHAPTER 1

One United People

PEK SIOK LIAN

When I was first asked to chair this panel discussion on the topic, "One United People", I ran it past some friends to get their opinion. "Aren't Singaporeans a pretty united bunch?" was the typical reaction from my non-Singaporean friends. "No one's hurling bombs at churches here. There are no demonstrations to speak of. What's the worry?"

My fellow Singaporeans were more "classic" (as we say here in Singapore) in their reaction: "What's there to discuss? We are all so passive and apathetic to start with. United or not united, you think we are going to start any fights? No point, *lah!*"

Frankly, both reactions are not too far off the mark. Most agree the Singapore government has, over the last 40 years, managed to organise our diverse populace into a relatively unified people. The Maria Hertogh riots, which saw Muslims protesting a court decision to give custody of a 13-year-old Dutch girl to her biological Catholic parents after she had been raised as a Muslim under foster care, are now a page in the history books — purely academic. The younger generation has at best, a hazy impression of what transpired in 1950.

From the age of six, our kids start declaring that we are "one united people regardless of race, language or religion." And somehow, over the years, in our efforts to stay united, sensitive, respectful and secular, we have religiously avoided talking about anything to do with race or religion. "Too sensitive." "Better not discuss." "OB!" These are just some of the typical reactions we hear. And then, there is also the tacit social contract where freedom of speech characteristic of a Western-style democracy is set aside for the practical goal of improving material conditions for the collective good.

This is a pragmatism that has propelled us to where we are today. Hence the second common reaction: "No point talking, let's just get on with things even if we're not entirely happy."

Fast forward to 2010, a brand new decade and a brand new year, with brand new Singaporeans. About 1.5 million new immigrants, citizens, permanent residents and foreigners have joined us here on this tropical island in the past few years. So it is not surprising that we now find ourselves thrust into another round of national soul-searching. With an extra million or so people in the mix, hailing from countries as diverse as China, Indonesia, India, Malaysia, Burma and Vietnam, what in the world do we mean now when we say "One United People"?

For instance, I have friends from India who, when they first came to live and work here in Singapore, said: "Singapore is a fantastic city. In fact, it is the best Indian city!" It is a huge compliment, obviously, but you see what defines their sense of home. By the way, if you think they are all hanging out in Little India, think again. They are more likely to be found in Clarke Quay, which some have dubbed Little India 2.0, thanks to the Rupee Room pumping out Shah Rukh Khan hits, as well as a whole host of other establishments catering to these new arrivals.

Did you also know that we have a new Chinatown? It has sprung up in our very own red-light district of Geylang where a growing number of Chinese nationals — businessmen and students, as well as people who work in restaurants, reflexology shops, construction — are making their home. Just take a walk there any one of these evenings and you will hear many different Chinese dialects and see lots of shops with Chinese-only signs and scores of Chinese workers sitting along the streets unwinding after a hard day's work.

With these new residents creating their own social enclaves, what is percolating now in our petri-dish experiment of social harmony? Are the new Mohicans (to borrow the words of Minister Mentor Lee Kuan Yew) going to get on with the old Mohicans? Are the original Singaporeans going to play nice? Are they getting resentful or ungracious? There have certainly been grumblings about why these new Singaporeans do not have to do National Service, do not bother to learn English to assimilate and how they are taking our jobs and driving up real estate prices.

No doubt, new interest groups are emerging in this changing social landscape which makes the task of strengthening our social fabric all that more pressing. The key challenge here is to satisfy all of our aspirations as Singapore becomes home to more people. Herein lies the task for each and every one of us today: to help rethink, rework and redefine the current practices and policies designed to deliver the cherished ideal of "One United People".

CHAPTER 2

The Third Phase of Singapore's Multiculturalism

DANIEL PS GOH

In 2003, Minister Yaacob Ibrahim made a landmark speech envisioning the third phase of Singapore's multiculturalism as combining and going beyond the melting pot and mosaic approaches of the first two phases. Starting from the attainment of self-government in the 1950s, the first phase involved the nation-building promotion of multiracial harmony and construction of a Singaporean identity through the enlargement of the area where Chinese, Malay, Indian and other cultural beliefs and practices overlapped. In the 1980s, as the effects of Westernisation were felt with successful capitalist development, emphasis was shifted to the construction of hyphenated Chinese-Singaporean, Malay-Singaporean, Indian-Singaporean identities to encourage the retention of ethnic culture. In the current third phase, as globalisation brings with it cultural diversity, cross-cultural understanding and dialogue are encouraged to foster hybrid Singaporean identities that would bind Singaporeans in a lattice of shared cultural links, grounded in the heartland and spreading out into the cosmopolitan world.

It is not an easy task to combine the melting-pot and mosaic approaches and yet foster hybrid identities. In principle, the promotion of racial and religious harmony can complement ethnic heritage preservation. One can develop a deep appreciation and actively practise one's own cultural heritage while exercising tolerance of other cultures. Indeed, sociologists have demonstrated that the individual who preserves his or her own cultural heritage is better equipped to appreciate, understand and adopt other cultures. If hybridity involves the fusion of two cultures to create unique shared cultures, then it makes sense that one must have a culture to share and fuse with other cultures to begin with. Institutionally, in Singapore, the same individual can be involved in the cultural exchange programs at the local community centre, volunteer to help his or her own cultural kin at the self-help groups Mendaki, the Chinese Development Assistance Council (CDAC) or the Singapore Indian Development Association (SINDA) and participate in cross-cultural dialogues in an Inter-Racial and Religious Confidence Circle (IRCC) without feeling torn or conflicted. The problem does not lie at the level of individuals or the institutions themselves, but at the level of the public sphere. The public sphere lies between individuals and the state. It is the civic space where individuals interact with each other and produce public opinions, shared cultural values and the social practices of citizenship. This is the space where society is created and trust, the glue that binds society together, is cultivated. Multiculturalism describes the principles and norms of intercultural interaction that have been established in the public sphere. Individuals form associations and organisations to act as a group in the public sphere, creating what we call civil society.

In Singapore, the state has intervened heavily in the public sphere and influenced its multiculturalism through state institutions such as community centres, ethnic self-help groups and confidence circles for good reason. Colonial civil society was largely commercially- and philanthropy-oriented, with only a few associations geared towards cultural modernisation. New multicultural institutions were urgently needed in the 1950s to replace the vicious colonial circle of racial divide-and-rule with a nation-building one. In the 1980s, another set of institutions was called for to substitute the virtuous circle of heritage preservation with the capitalist circle of consumerist individualism. We have been relatively successful, but the unintended consequence has been the creation of a new vicious circle that undermines the multicultural dialogues and hybrid identities that are needed to maintain social cohesion in the age of globalisation. To make my case, I will use examples from my observations of the Racial and Religious Harmony Carnivals in Punggol town, my experiences teaching the sociology of race relations to undergraduates and my observations of recent events concerning race and religious relations in Singapore. I do this without prejudice to the local grassroots volunteers and Member of Parliament in Punggol, my students and other individuals. The problem cannot be tackled on the level of the individual, but must be a concerted effort at the level of the public sphere. I conclude by proposing eight principles that could be followed to break this new vicious circle and realise genuine multicultural dialogues.[1]

MAKING VIRTUOSITY OF COLONIAL RACIALISM

In the early 1950s, in the midst of the propaganda war against the communists during the Emergency, the Malayan Director of Information Services outlined his approach to citizenship education: to teach the new citizens of a nascent Malaya to understand "how the wheel goes round, who keeps it in motion, and the part played by Ahmad, Ah Seng and Ramasamy in its revolution". The how and who, of course, refer to the colonial state. The three characters were caricatures emblematic of British colonial racialism in Malaya and were predecessors of the Chinese, Malay and Indian figures that dominate our multicultural imagination today. Colonial rule was built on the hard racial divisions institutionalised in politics and the economy. Racial segregation and pluralism were the order of the day, allowing for a handful of white colonialists to rule over a large native population. In British Malaya, the Chinese, viewed as apolitical economic animals and long treated as aliens in a country they were increasingly calling their own, were kept out of the bureaucracy and the military. The Malays were treated as a highly conservative people protective of their traditions, so many were therefore kept in their fields and cajoled and coerced to plant only rice and vegetables, while the Malays of noble birth were inducted by

---

[1] For smoother reading, I have decided not to pepper this article with notes and academic references. For fuller academic expositions of my arguments with proper referencing of the academic literature, please see Daniel PS Goh, "Colonial Pluralism, Nationalism and Postcolonial Multiculturalism: Race and the Question of Cultural Diversity in Malaysia and Singapore," *Sociology Compass*, 2008, vol. 2, no. 1, pp. 232–52; "Multiculturalism and the Problem of Solidarity in Singapore," in Terence Chong (ed.), *Singapore: Management of Success Revisited*, Singapore: Institute of Southeast Asian Studies, 2010, forthcoming, and with Philip Holden, "Introduction: Postcoloniality, Race and Multiculturalism," in Goh *et al.* (eds.), *Race and Multiculturalism in Malaysia and Singapore*, London: Routledge, 2009, pp. 1–16.

the British into the bureaucracy and the military because they identified with fellow aristocrats. Indian migrants were specially "imported" into two classes — the supposedly docile Tamils as plantation workers and manual labourers and the well-schooled Indians as white-collar clerks.

Caught up in the institutionalised segregation, the socialised behaviour of the different races easily became racial stereotypes and these were taken as natural inborn attributes. The Malays who preferred planting to hard mining labour were said to be lazy sons of the soil. The Chinese, seeking every opportunity to earn a living, were said to be irredeemably greedy, scheming and untrustworthy. The Tamils suffering in the isolated plantations under powerful European masters were said to be uncivilised, childlike and naïve. The British officials wrote extensively of these attributes as justifications for colonial racial policy. Hence, the caricatures of Ahmad, Ah Seng and Ramasamy also represent the colonial racial stereotypes that still thrive today in the undercurrent of prejudices beneath the calm surface of racial harmony.

The Vicious Circle of Colonial Racialism

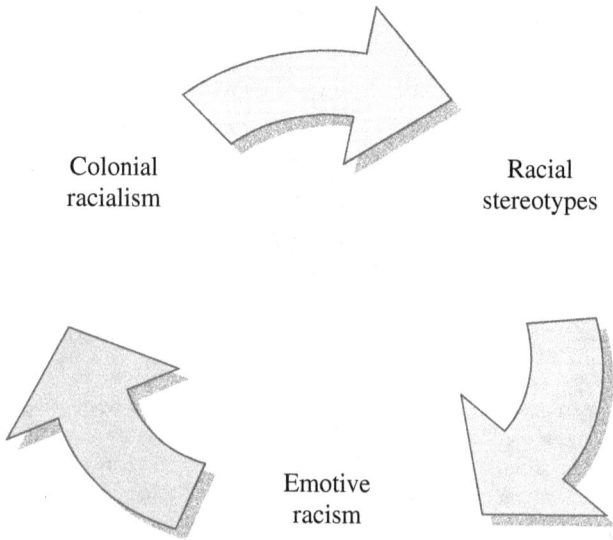

Colonial
racialism

Racial
stereotypes

Emotive
racism

Figure 1 Vicious circles are also often self-fulfilling prophecies

22

These prejudices have erupted three times as racial riots — in 1950, 1964 and 1969. There is no need for me to repeat the well-trodden history of the riots, except to say that the racial stereotypes offered a dangerously rich pool of emotions and symbolisms for unscrupulous politicians to exploit and turn into emotionally charged racist acts for their own gain. The strife was also underpinned by the economic competition between the races, with the stereotypes playing a key role in overt and covert discrimination, thus adding emotional fuel to racism. In turn, this emotional racism affirmed the "truth" of colonial racialism — that race is a "primordial" fact and races should be kept apart and race relations managed by strong government.

The first phase of multiculturalism attempted to transform the vicious circle into a virtuous one. The melting pot multiculturalism envisioned by then-Minister of Culture S. Rajaratnam accepted the colonial racial divisions as hard facts. Thus, Chinese, Malay, Indian and the residual category of Others (CMIO) were said to be constituent races of Singapore and were represented by discrete, closed circles. Rajaratnam's ingenious adaptation was to make these self-contained circles overlap by arguing that there was a common shared cultural space between all of them. The enlargement of this space through government-sponsored campaigns and institutions would therefore bring about a unifying Singaporean national culture. In this sense, the terms of colonial racialism were accepted but transformed into postcolonial multiracialism. It was a pragmatic solution, as colonial racialism was already deeply embedded in the population, in institutionalised economic practices, in people's minds as stereotypes and in people's hearts as emotional prejudices.

Today, postcolonial multiracialism continues to be a major cue in organising the grassroots activities in the public sphere. Each year, on the weekend close to Racial Harmony Day, the informational flyer advertising the Racial and Religious Harmony Carnival in Punggol shows children, decked out in ethnic costumes representing the CMIO races, posing with government ministers and Members of Parliament. Carnival activities follow the CMIO representation. Residents visiting the exhibition on cultural heritage will find themselves learning about Chinese, Malay, Indian and Eurasian or Peranakan customs and can take part in a quiz to earn prizes. Educational stalls set up by invited religious groups will definitely include a

Buddhist or Taoist temple, a mosque, a Hindu temple and a church in the area. Food stalls offer free *halal*-certified CMIO cuisines for all to sample and share. The carnival parade itself is also structured as such, with different schools offering a menu of traditional Chinese, Malay, Indian and Eurasian cuisines and modern dances choreographed in different combinations.

Overall, the activities offer positive cultural stereotypes to replace the negative stereotypes of colonial racialism. For example, Indians are associated with saris, Bollywood music, tandoori chicken, henna hand-painting and Hinduism. And the primary mode of interaction here is cultural exchange. Thus, we find Chinese and Malay children getting their hands painted and sampling tandoori chicken. The result is a sense of emotional bonding through cultural exchange, which replaces the racist emotions of colonial racialism. In this way, the shared cultural space is gradually enlarged and postcolonial multiracialism realised.

The Virtuous Circle of Postcolonial Multiracialism

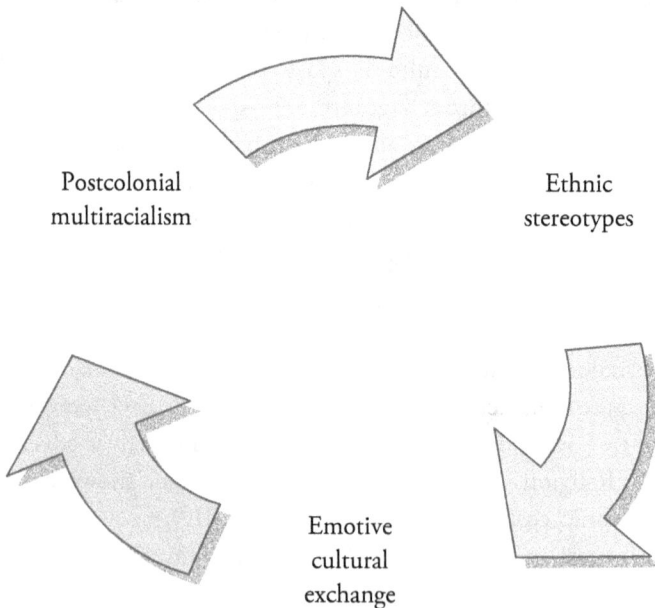

Postcolonial
multiracialism

Ethnic
stereotypes

Emotive
cultural
exchange

Figure 2 The virtuous circle of postcolonial multiracialism may be realised by gradually enlarging the shared cultural space

MAKING VIRTUOSITY OF CONSUMER CAPITALISM

By the end of the 1970s, with successful industrialisation and Singapore well on its way to becoming a fasting-developing "Asian Tiger", another set of problems presented itself. Because of Singapore's open economy and close economic linkages with the West, particularly the United States, capitalism came with strong cultural baggage. Before economic modernisation, consumption cultures were limited to the "leisure classes" — the propertied and capitalist classes who displayed their status through luxury lifestyles and conspicuous mass consumption invented in early twentieth-century America and accelerated in the postwar era. Consumer capitalism promised the common folk a wide range of cheap goods and comfortable materialist living. Every hardworking American could get easy credit, own a suburban home, buy a car, drive to shop at the neighbourhood supermarket and departmental stores filled with goods from all over the world and take a vacation every summer holiday. American mass consumption supported the global capitalist economy but also promoted and universalised this American Dream.

Today, we do not think much of the American Dream because we have our own version of the Singapore Dream — the 5Cs, representing condominium, car, country club, credit card and cash. Today, consumerism has become a basic aspect of Singaporean culture and the national pastime is quite obviously shopping. But, it must have been a strange thing taking root in Singapore in the 1970s. While the Singapore government's home ownership scheme allowed the majority of Singaporeans to own their own homes, like Americans, the Singapore scheme was and is a public housing programme with socialist underpinnings. As an export-oriented economy, consumerism was seen as irrelevant at best and a distraction that detracted from productivity and reduced the savings rate at worst. The worry was that a consumption culture, once taken root, would pave the way for excessive runaway consumerism that would undermine the newly built economic success of the country. Very quickly, a situation arose that sociologists call "moral panic": the fear that political, economic and social change would spell the collapse of morality, civilisation and society itself. Excessive consumerism, it was feared, would encourage selfish individualism and destroy the nuclear family household that had been the basis of governmental social policy. It was believed that the nuclear family performed the function of transmitting moral values to the next generation and it was feared that the traditional Chinese family, in particular, was under threat. The precedent for this moral panic could be found in the anti-"yellow culture" campaigns advocated in the 1960s by the Chinese-speaking intelligentsia who associated bourgeois decadence with Western individualism.

The Vicious Circle of Consumer Capitalism

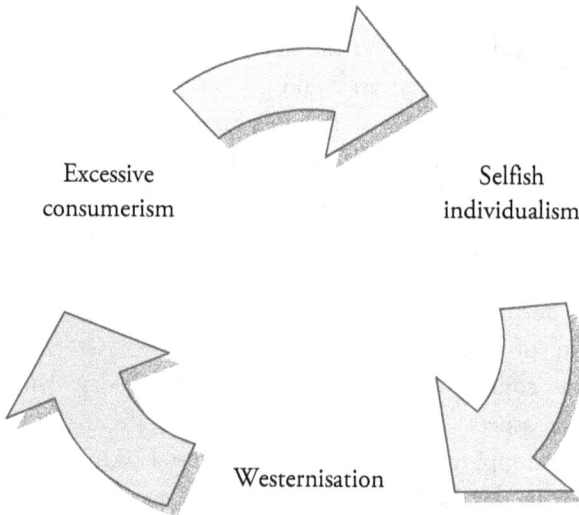

Excessive consumerism

Selfish individualism

Westernisation

Figure 3 In the 1970s, the vicious circle of excessive consumerism, selfish individualism and Westernisation threatened not only the industrialising economy and moral society, but also the nascent nation

To make matters worse, individualism had taken on a more sinister shade in the late 1970s because its association with Westernisation portended the erosion of the values of the CMIO cultures that had been the building blocks of postcolonial multiracialism. It was feared that, released from the moorings of ethnic culture, the nation-building project would collapse and racial and religious strife would return. Intensifying economic competition was also leading to unequal outcomes for the races and it became apparent that Malay and Indian children were disproportionately over-represented among the underachievers in school. Therefore, for government leaders then, the vicious circle of excessive consumerism, selfish individualism and Westernisation threatened not only the industrialising economy and moral society, but also the very nation that was just being born.

The 1980s saw the creation of many institutional innovations aimed at shoring up ethnic culture and tackling the consequences of successful capitalist development. Goh Keng Swee, then-Deputy Prime Minister, introduced moral and religious education in schools. The Prime Minister, Lee Kuan Yew, launched the Speak Mandarin Campaign by switching from Hokkien to Mandarin in his National Day Rally speech. The Special Assistance Plan (SAP) program converted some elite schools into specialised schools for Chinese language and cultural education. Confucian ethics were promoted and academic specialists were invited to write textbooks and set up a research institute on the subject. The Malay self-help group Mendaki was established and became the template for other ethnic self-help groups to follow. The Ethnic Integration Policy and the Group Representation Constituency were set up to ensure proportional ethnic mixing in public housing estates and proportional ethnic representation in Parliament respectively. Parliament enshrined a set of shared Asian values in the National Ideology.

These institutional innovations replaced individualism with communitarianism and Westernisation with "Asianisation". As a result, excessive consumerism and conspicuous consumption were soon frowned upon as unbecoming of an Asian society and immoral, while community service and the development of the philanthropic spirit were encouraged. Consumerism was not eradicated; it cannot be in an open capitalist economy. Consumerism was instead moderated and Asianised, and as such, deployed in the service of multiracialism.

The Punggol Racial and Religious Harmony Carnival is immersed in the trappings of consumption culture. On top of publicity materials on community service work, most of the religious educational stalls offer suitably ethnic free food, drinks and gifts. One can get Indian sweets at the Hindu temple booth, soya bean milk and grass jelly drink at the Taoist temple booth, vegetarian vermicelli and spring rolls at the Buddhist temple booth, and fruit chocolate fondue and balloon sculptures at a Christian church booth. The parade seems almost like a sideshow alongside the food and funfair, but the manning of the stalls by grassroots volunteers who fairly apportion the free food affirm both communitarian spirit and moderated consumerism. Even McDonald's, the epitome of Western consumerism, which gives out free drinks and burgers, takes on a communitarian and Asian flavour here. At its booth, an exhibition panel features a cast of multiracial employees, highlighting McDonald's as a community-oriented, family-like and equal-opportunity employer.

The Virtuous Circle of Communitarian Capitalism

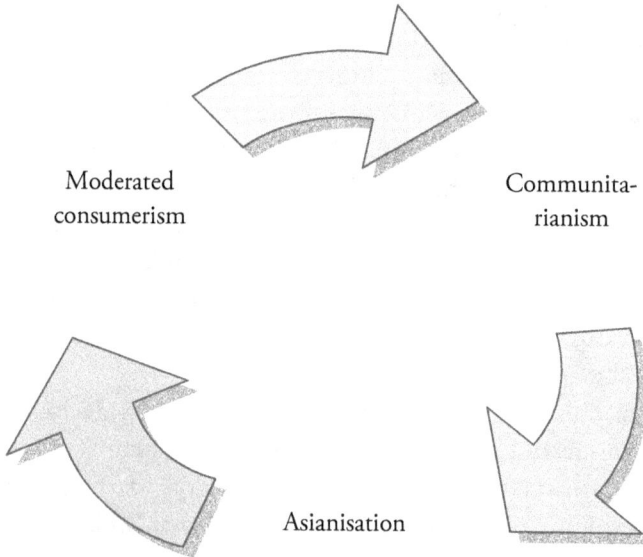

Moderated
consumerism

Communita-
rianism

Asianisation

Figure 4 Individualism, Westernisation and excessive consumerism were countered by an attempt at Asianisation, moderated consumerism and communitarianism

DIALOGUE VERSES THE VICIOUS CIRCLE OF FEAR

Compared to the first phase and its emphasis on shared common space, the second phase of multiculturalism brought racial and religious differences to the foreground of the public sphere and into the calculations of governmental policies and social interactions alike. As such, the institutional innovations opened up a Pandora's Box of heightened racial and religious consciousness in the public sphere. This is not necessarily a bad thing, as the search for commonalities can only be achieved through frank discussions and debates about differences. However, the government eventually closed the Box by enacting the Maintenance of Religious Harmony Act and began to define hard "out-of-bounds markers" for the public discussion of racial and religious issues. This has led to hypersensitivity and much self-censorship in the public sphere.

When I discuss issues of racial prejudice, stereotypes and institutional racism and give Singaporean examples in lectures, students are often visibly uncomfortable with me openly talking about a subject they think is highly sensitive. Once, after a lecture, a Chinese–Singaporean student emailed me at length to tell me that I should be more sensitive to the Malays in class and not try to explain sociologically why Malays are disproportionately underachieving in school. She spoke for Malay classmates that she did not know and claimed that they were upset without finding out whether they actually were. She informed me that she interned with a newspaper and implied that she could report this if she wanted. Another time, I had to intervene after Chinese–Singaporean students emailed to complain about their Malay tutor bringing up hard questions about racial prejudices and discrimination in Singapore and threatened to make a complaint in the press and to the authorities. Even in smaller tutorial classes, it is much more difficult to get students to talk about racial and religious issues than about other issues.

These are university students who should be open in their thinking and challenging conventional understandings in the scientific search for truth. Yet, many have proven to be unable to overcome their conditioning to be hypersensitive. They would rather not discuss racial or religious issues because they are afraid of offending someone, as they are hypersensitive and will take offence themselves. Because they do not discuss racial or religious issues, over time, they will lose their capacity to talk and use their reasoning to disentangle the issues. Postcolonial multiracialism and Asianisation do not help either. Students conditioned by activities such as the Punggol carnival remain stuck within the CMIO framework and cannot imagine multicultural possibilities beyond it. Emotional cultural exchange encourages them to trade superficial details about customs that many do not even practise anymore, and the emotional component further encourages hypersensitivity. For them, multiculturalism refers to the consumption of other Asian cuisines, the moderated consumerism of the second phase. It is significant that Minister Yaacob used the example of people of different races eating vegetarian food at Komala Vilas in Little India to exemplify hybridity in his 2003 speech.

What disturbs me most is the patronising attitude that some of my Chinese students adopt towards their non-Chinese classmates. They do not check with their classmates on how they are feeling before purporting to know that they are uncomfortable and arrogantly speaking on their behalf. They assume that their non-Chinese classmates are narrow-minded and hypersensitive and have not considered that they may have projected their own discomfort on their classmates. In the case of the complaint against my tutor, I surveyed the rest of the students in the class. Most told me that they had appreciated the discussion although they had felt uncomfortable while

The Vicious Circle of Fear and Self-censorship

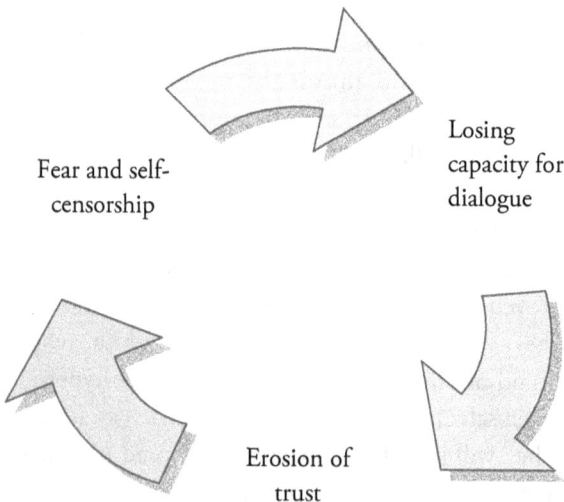

Fear and self-censorship

Losing capacity for dialogue

Erosion of trust

Figure 5 The vicious circle, if allowed to spiral, will undermine the racial and religious dialogue that is being promoted in the third phase of multiculturalism

the rest were angered by the patronising attitude of the complaining students. This is highly disturbing because it shows the erosion of trust among Singaporeans, to the extent that the leading members of the Chinese majority feel an obligation to represent the non-Chinese minorities and protect them paternalistically against "sensitive" comments by reporting matters to the authorities. They cannot even trust themselves or their fellow Singaporeans to talk about the matter as reasonable individuals. If this process continues, the racial and religious dialogue that is being promoted in the third phase of multiculturalism will be short-circuited.

Two recent events show clearly the operation of this vicious circle of fear and self-censorship. Early this year, McDonald's launched its Chinese Zodiac Doraemon doll series. However, the company replaced the pig doll with a Cupid doll, explaining to customers that it could not sell pig dolls because it was a *halal*-certified restaurant. The move backfired when some Chinese customers protested and even blamed Muslims for being oversensitive and intolerant of Chinese culture. The company then tried to fudge the issue by claiming that the series was not a Chinese Zodiac series after all, despite the fact that, with the pig reinstated, it would have contained all 12 animals of the Chinese Zodiac. Also, Singaporeans soon realised that McDonald's was selling a complete set in Hong Kong, with the pig. This led to more protests and the incident quickly became a media event. The company eventually apologised and brought back the pig into the series.

This incident not only shows a general lack of cross-cultural understanding, but also the lack of capacity for dialogue, both of which have important consequences in a globalised Singapore. McDonald's could have avoided the whole fiasco if the company had consulted Muslim leaders and scholars, who would have told the company that Muslims do not mind pig toys and would even buy them for their kids to play with. Instead, it chose to go the route of hypersensitivity and self-censorship and, even when questioned, was not capable of engaging in dialogue with the public, acting instead in a seemingly patronising manner towards Muslims and non-Muslims alike. The company eventually made a graceful public apology to end the saga. But the damage had been done as the incident made Muslims look insensitive and the Chinese too defensive of their customs, thus further eroding the trust quotient of society.

Very recently, the Internal Security Department called up and warned Pastor Rony Tan of a large Christian mega-church to be mindful of religious sensitivity. Tan had ridiculed and belittled Buddhism at length during a Sunday service and a video clip was posted on the church website which spread quickly and created a huge uproar on the Internet. At the time of writing, the event is still being played out, but the response to Tan's grave mistake is already telling. While many wrote to Pastor Tan to communicate their disagreement and disapproval in the proper spirit of multicultural dialogue, enough citizens complained to the authorities and made police reports, causing the Department to act in a public manner to calm things down. Tan made a public apology and a personal apology to Buddhist leaders and promised that he would get involved in inter-religious dialogue after the governmental warning. But the element of fear and self-censorship still hangs over the event. It would have been more reassuring if he had apologised because a multi-religious group of community leaders went to talk to him. Or perhaps the Inter-Racial and Religious Confidence Circles could have made Pastor Tan see that he was wrong, thereby restoring public confidence in our multicultural system. Using a sledgehammer to crack a nut is counterproductive. Thus, despite Tan's apology, some citizens are still calling for him to be arrested and a few religious leaders want the authorities to ensure that this will not happen again. This erosion of social trust means the government has to constantly be on guard to police racial and religious relations and step in with the threat of force to resolve disputes, which in turn reinforces a climate of fear and hypersensitivity and reduces dialogue to a minimum.

BUILDING MULTICULTURAL CAPACITY

There is a glimmer of hope yet for the third phase. The international World Values Survey shows that Singapore ranks very poorly among Asian countries in terms of social trust and participation in political discussions. Yet, when asked what the country should prioritise, other than economic development, a larger percentage of Singaporeans want the government to give them more say, compared to citizens in other countries and other priorities.

Social Trust in Selected Asia-Pacific Countries

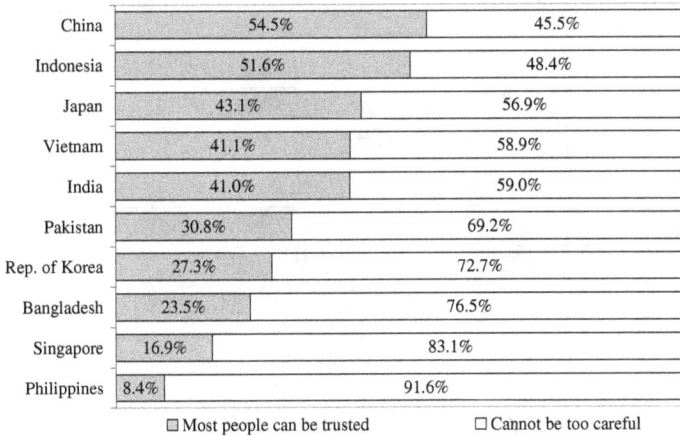

Country	Most people can be trusted	Cannot be too careful
China	54.5%	45.5%
Indonesia	51.6%	48.4%
Japan	43.1%	56.9%
Vietnam	41.1%	58.9%
India	41.0%	59.0%
Pakistan	30.8%	69.2%
Rep. of Korea	27.3%	72.7%
Bangladesh	23.5%	76.5%
Singapore	16.9%	83.1%
Philippines	8.4%	91.6%

☑ Most people can be trusted   ☐ Cannot be too careful

Figure 6 The 2000–2002 World Values Survey shows that among selected Asia-Pacific countries, Singapore society exhibits a relatively lower level of social trust
Source: World Values Survey, 2000–2002

Frequency of Discussion of Political Matters with Friends, Selected Asia-Pacific Countries

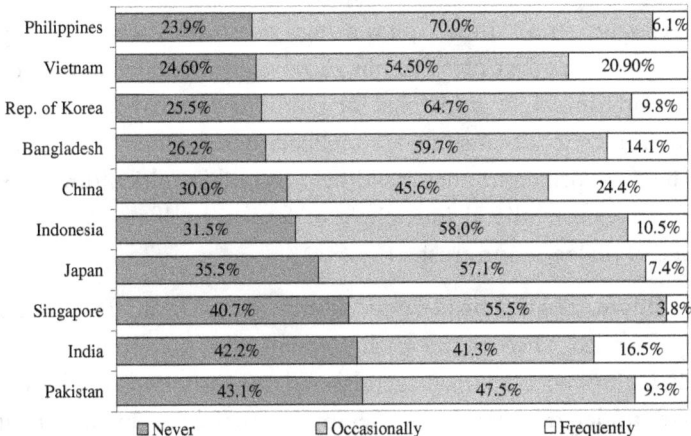

Country	Never	Occasionally	Frequently
Philippines	23.9%	70.0%	6.1%
Vietnam	24.60%	54.50%	20.90%
Rep. of Korea	25.5%	64.7%	9.8%
Bangladesh	26.2%	59.7%	14.1%
China	30.0%	45.6%	24.4%
Indonesia	31.5%	58.0%	10.5%
Japan	35.5%	57.1%	7.4%
Singapore	40.7%	55.5%	3.8%
India	42.2%	41.3%	16.5%
Pakistan	43.1%	47.5%	9.3%

■ Never   ☐ Occasionally   ☐ Frequently

Figure 7 Singapore also fares poorly in terms of how frequently they engage in discussions involving political issues with their friends
Source: World Values Survey, 2000–2002

Prioritise Democratic Development or Social Order?

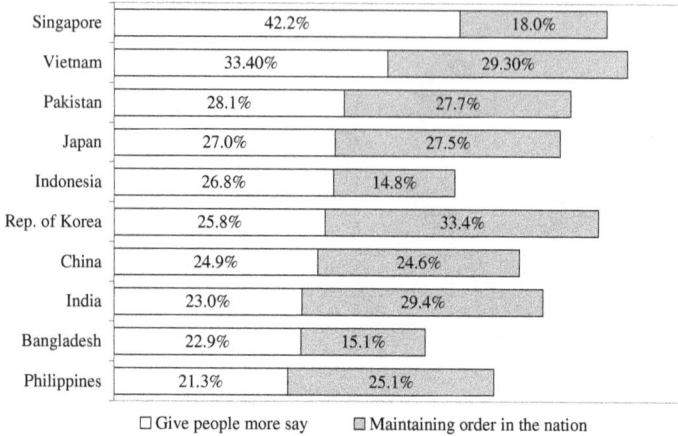

Country	Give people more say	Maintaining order in the nation
Singapore	42.2%	18.0%
Vietnam	33.40%	29.30%
Pakistan	28.1%	27.7%
Japan	27.0%	27.5%
Indonesia	26.8%	14.8%
Rep. of Korea	25.8%	33.4%
China	24.9%	24.6%
India	23.0%	29.4%
Bangladesh	22.9%	15.1%
Philippines	21.3%	25.1%

☐ Give people more say ☐ Maintaining order in the nation

Figure 8 Compared to some other countries surveyed, when asked to choose between the two, more Singaporeans favoured democratic development over the social order
Source: World Values Survey, 2000–2002

Just as we did in the first two phases of multiculturalism, we need to confront and transform the vicious circle that is now obstructing cross-cultural dialogue and, thus, preventing us from achieving hybrid Singaporean identities that preserve our social unity in a globalised world. I conclude by offering eight principles for public sphere participation that I draw from academic discussions on deliberative democracy and public spheres. These are principles that could help us build multicultural capacity and help us transform the vicious circle of fear and self-censorship into a virtuous one of dialogue and trust.

- **Facilitate, not frame:** leaders should act as facilitators of honest open-ended discussions rather than try to frame and limit discussions with political agendas and out-of-bounds markers.
- **Use understanding, not therapy:** participants in multicultural dialogue should use reasoning to seek the understanding of others and empathy to understand others, rather than resort to emotional outpourings and sympathy.

- **Be sensitive, not patronising**: participants should be sensitive in their phrasing but not so sensitive that they adopt a patronising attitude towards others.
- **Ethnicise, not racialise**: participants should focus on culture and recognise the possibility of creative cultural change and adoption rather than reduce behaviour to unchanging biological instincts.
- **Be relational, not communal**: participants should relate to each other as individuals with experiences and opinions to share rather than as communal or self-appointed representatives exercising authority.
- **Act, not react**: participants should be actively and continuously engaging in multicultural dialogue, rather than speaking up only in offensive or defensive reaction to an incident.
- **Consensus, not suppression**: participants should seek genuine consensus on views and norms, and working consensus on norms for tolerance and coexistence when differences are irreconcilable, rather than suppress differences.
- **Evaluate, not judge**: participants should evaluate cultural beliefs and practices using shared moral standards and should not judge and belittle them using their own ethnic or religious standards.

CHAPTER 3

Why *NEWater* Instead of *SE*Water: Difficult Policies and Unity for Singaporeans

LEONG CHING

NEWATER AND TOILET WATER

Once upon a time in 1997, two countries decided that they needed more water. One was experiencing the worst drought in a very long time, the other was held ransom by a neighbour who controlled its water supply. They both looked at the water flushed down their loos every day, discharged into the sea, and thought: "Hey! Why not recycle?" After all, people in one part of America have been doing it for years, and they look all right. Both countries, desperate for water, decided to give it a try. They planned carefully and took 12 years to think, consult and debate. One succeeded, the other did not.

When you think of the usual suspects that unify a country, you think, perhaps they all speak a common language like Japanese, or they share 5,000 years of history like China, or the people are of a particular race, or they are peculiarly locked into a geographical area and are relatively isolated from the world.

All these are, of course, stereotypical, especially in the modern world, but the nature of generalisations is that they are, generally, more or less, true. For Singapore, these parameters fail more spectacularly than usual.

Unless we count Singlish as a common language, in which case I, for one, would pass with flying colours.

Singaporeans do not have a long shared history, we do not have a common language that has been bred in our genes for generations and we are, of course, of different races. The search for one united people must start elsewhere. If we conclude that this unifying factor does not occur naturally, it must then be artificially constructed.

WHY GOOD STORIES MAKE GOOD POLICIES

This paper, which is part of my on-going PhD research at the Lee Kuan Yew School of Public Policy, is an exegesis of the notion of public policy as narrative, in particular, the idea that a policy has to fulfil criteria of truth, richness and coherence to be considered a good narrative. Or, more simply, why good stories make good policies. And how these public stories make Singaporeans one united people.

First, I will outline the process by which Singapore achieves very difficult policy change by using the case of NEWater. Pumping recycled water into the national drinking water supply is a politically difficult policy and one that a few other countries have tried unsuccessfully to implement. I shall use a comparison of the narratives between Singapore and Queensland, Australia, to show the difference in how the issue was constructed in the newspapers, and the impact this had on policy change. The analysis will show that the speed with which Singapore created policy knowledge made an impact on the success of the policy.

Second, I shall make a separate argument about what counts as a good narrative — how the variables of truth, richness and consistency matter.

Last, I shall tie these two strands together to form a narrative model of policy change. This model speaks about four types of change relating to narratives:

i.   Revolutionary change, where both the extent of change and the strength of the narratives are high (an example of which would be the recycled water policy in Singapore)

ii.   An experimentation stage, either where a country is preparing for some large change or has fallen back from an unsuccessful revolutionary change (for example, the case of Toowoomba in

Queensland, which tried to implement a water reuse policy but did not succeed).

iii.   Political incrementalism, a policy change that is in actual fact a very small change in reality but has been amplified for political ends

iv.   Technical incrementalism, the business-as-usual policy changes that we see day to day.

A note about the title: why NEWater instead of SEWater? (Short for sewage water, which is factually as true?) The difference shows how narratives and framing are important. In Queensland, even leaders that supported the change urged the people to drink "toilet water". In Singapore, the politicians presented a more consistent image. In short, the narrative was stronger, enabling them to quickly build a consensus.

INTRODUCTION

Singapore has managed to implement many policies which appear to be controversial and intractable in other countries. Its high ministerial pay, its electronic road pricing system and its drinking water supply. Such difficult policies can be successfully implemented because there is an unusually high degree of unity of purpose among Singaporeans with regards to public policies (as distinct from politics). Without widespread public acceptance and social cohesion, such difficult policies would fail, as they have in many other countries. Now, my argument is silent on whether or not these are in fact good policies — it is merely that these are intractable, politically-difficult policies that have been successfully implemented. It might very well be that this unity among Singaporeans stems from that fact that we are united in common misery over these policies — what is more common among Singaporeans than complaining about the Electronic Road Pricing system? How does this unity of purpose come about? In this paper, when I speak of national unity, I will do so in a fairly neutral way — as a broad consensus to adopt a certain way forward to deal with a national problem.

SINGAPORE AND AUSTRALIA: COMPARABLE?

In a word, yes — in a very limited way. Yes, if we look in terms of Australia's shortage of water, and in terms of its attempt to implement a particular solution. I realise of course that there are many things that are different about the two countries — political culture, the sheer size, history and policy-making regimes. However, if we just look at the water sector and how the narrative turns out, I think we might find it a useful exercise, despite the difference.

Since gaining independence in 1965, Singapore has been dependent on its neighbour Malaysia for much of its water supply. Over the past four decades, the two countries have experienced periods of good and bad bilateral relations. Despite the signing of two long-term water agreements, the issue of water security has not been fully settled.

In 1997, Singapore publicly stated that it was aggressively looking at alternative sources of water. This was precipitated by difficulties with Malaysia over the price of raw water, with the Malaysians threatening to increase prices by at least six times and with no set formula to peg to future increases.

In 1998, Singapore began studying wastewater as a source of raw water. The water would go through a purification and treatment process using membrane and ultraviolet technologies. Drinking water would be produced by a procedure known as Planned Indirect Potable Use (or Planned IPU). Three years later, the reused water was ready for non-potable use — for wafer fabrication processes, non-potable applications in manufacturing processes, as well as for air-conditioning cooling towers in commercial buildings.

In 2003, the reused water, named NEWater, was introduced into water reservoirs. The amount made up about 1% of total daily water consumption in 2009 and will be increased progressively to about 2.5% of total daily water consumption by 2011.

At around the same time, Australia experienced the same sense of crisis. At the time, it was facing a chronic water shortage due to drought and below-average rainfalls. The Queensland State Government initiated the Caloundra/Maroochy Strategic Wastewater Management Strategy, including plans to introduce reused water into the drinking supply. The Queensland State Government also initiated the Queensland Water Recycling Strategy (QWRS).

One of the most drought-stricken communities was Toowoomba in south-east Queensland. In 2006, the government held a referendum to recycle waste water for drinking water supplies. In reaction, a group of citizens collected some 10,000 signatures for a petition opposing the project. In the referendum, residents of Toowoomba voted against the wastewater scheme. Today, the issue of water reuse remains high on Australia's national agenda — not surprisingly as it is the driest inhabited continent in the world.

"YUCK! I CAN'T DRINK THIS"

Figure 1 shows the analysis of some newspaper articles covering the period between 1997 and 2008. The reports were taken from five major Australian newspapers: *The Australian, The Courier Mail, The Sydney Morning Herald, The Age,* and *The West Australian.* In Singapore, the search terms used were: "recycled water, NEWater and desalination" covering the period of 1997–2008. Reports were taken from the three major English newspapers in Singapore, i.e., *The Straits Times, The Business Times,* and *The New Paper.* In the case of both locations, each report was tagged according to whether they were supportive of water reuse (positive), hostile to it (negative) or neither (neutral).

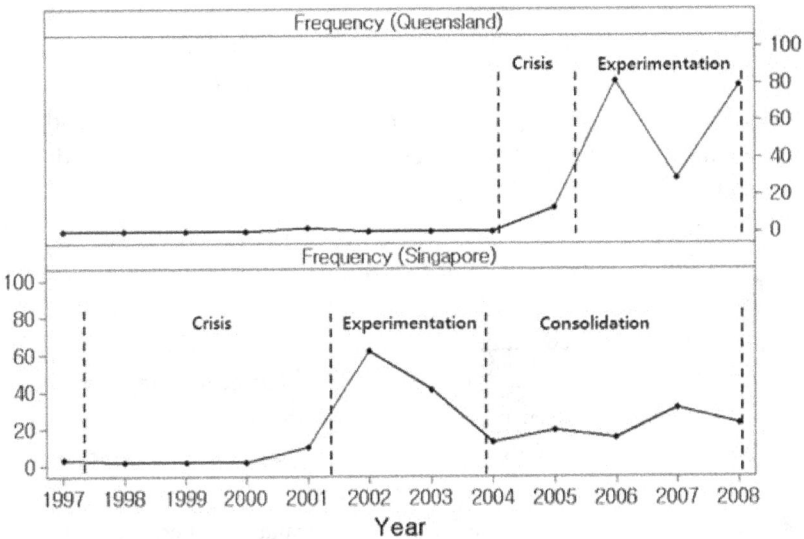

Figure 1 Analysis of newspaper coverage of recycled water

The "yuck" factor, the psychological reaction to drinking waste water, has often been seen to be an important factor in the success of recycled water policies. So, the stories were also examined to see whether and how they portrayed "yuck", a negative reaction, and how this impacted on the slant of the story as a whole. Public opinion was also tagged. Now, with some fairly simple regressions, we see that there is a quicker consolidation of views in Singapore compared to Australia.

A time trend analysis shows that there are three distinct stages in the media coverage of both countries, which are depicted in Figure 1. For both countries, media coverage on water reuse, which started slowly, gained momentum, and then peaked before stabilising. This demonstrates quite clearly the stages of institutional change, which reflect Harvard professor Pepper Culpepper's framework of "crisis, experimentation and consolidation". Culpepper says that during normal times, entrenched institutions are not easily displaced. During crises, however, a large number of players or actors upset the "cognitive bases" for such institutions.

The search then begins for a new equilibrium. Such experimentation is characterised by a deep uncertainty which places a premium on persuasive argument to create new knowledge.

Referring to Culpepper's framework again, where crises are seen as "common knowledge events" leading to the "emergence of shared ideas", so we have seen here that during crises there is creation of knowledge and an accelerated rate of learning. In this sense, it is easier to turn the tide of public opinion if the tide is still young.

This sets the stage for our discussion of media coverage over the years. As shown in Figure 1, media interest began building up between 1997 and 2001 and then peaked in 2002, before a gradual decline for Singapore. For Queensland, little media coverage existed between 2001 and 2005 and then suddenly it peaked in 2006 and again in 2008. Hence, for Singapore, the first "crisis phase" can be seen in 1997–2001. In this phase, the stories were overwhelmingly positive, with 84% of the reports on the topic being positive and none being negative.

On the other hand, in the same phase in Australia, the media perception was neutral in Queensland: 53% of the reports were positive and 33% negative. Given this, therefore, we see that the media representation of the issue during the early phase may have a significant impact for norm-formation. This is observed by contrasting the proportions of negative and positive mentions of 'yuck' — Yuck-Negative and Yuck-Positive — before the media interest peaks for the two countries.

That is just the quantitative way of saying: the story matters. It may be useful to look at some actual samples of stories. In Australia, some of the vocabulary used included "treated effluent", 'toilet to tap' and 'shit water', the latter used even by politicians who were actually supportive of the scheme. There was a confusing use of negative terms to describe reused water even by leaders who *supported* the cause. Australia's *Sydney Morning Herald* pointed out in 2005: "It doesn't help when politicians, both for and against recycling water, confuse the debate by suggesting people will be drinking human waste."

POLICY AS NARRATIVE

The idea of policy as narrative has developed in two ways. First, there are those who have argued that policy change needs to be understood in terms of *discourse* coalitions. These scholars have three main strands of argue. First, they say we need to understand the issue qualitatively, as well as in numbers. American scholar Frank Fisher for example says, "It is not knowledge in belief systems *per se* that holds members of collations together, but storylines. Unlike beliefs these cannot be analysed quantitatively only understood qualitatively." Second, there is sometimes a non-logical structure to the policy. That is to say, rather than a core of cognitive commitments, there are different stories that may sometimes be vague and contradictory. Third, reality is not an objective "given" but one which is normatively constituted.

The second way in which the idea of narrative has developed is to look at the internal criteria of what makes a good or bad narrative (and by extension a good or bad policy) One candidate for the narrative element is Thomas Kaplan's criteria of a "true, rich and consistent, coherent and unified" entity. This works roughly along the lines of a "true, justified belief" which some philosophers call "knowledge". So, now we have some elements of a theory of narratives which accounts for knowledge formation in policy making.

Degree of Change

	Revolutionary Change	Political Incrementalism
Narrative Strength	Experimentation	Technical Incrementalism

Figure 2 A narrative model of policy change

So we have a matrix of change. For example, in revolutionary change, because knowledge formation is relatively strong, both the extent of change and the strength of the narratives are high. An example of this would be the NEWater policy, which took more than two decades to come into fruition. There is also an account for an experimentation stage, either where a country is preparing for some large change or has fallen back from an unsuccessful revolutionary change. For example, there is the case of Toowoomba, which tried to implement a water reuse policy but did not succeed. The intended policy change was large but the narrative was confused.

Political incrementalism is a policy change that is. In actual fact, a very small change in reality but has been amplified for political ends; and technical incrementalism, the business-as-usual policy changes that we see day to day.

CONCLUSION

Unity is therefore not in the realm of politics but also policy. It is a matter of the mind, as well as the heart. I have argued that what unifies Singapore is a matter of our public policies, and the creation of public knowledge that goes with the process. A key part of this is the development of the national narrative which must speak sufficiently strongly to carry the ground in the case of difficult policies such as the introduction of recycled water.

CHAPTER 4

Reasonable Persons of Goodwill: Personal Experiences Navigating Diversity

AARON MANIAM

THREE STORIES

I am Singaporean, with a half-Indian, half-Eurasian father; a half-Pakistani, half-Malay mother. Dad converted to Islam from Roman Catholicism, so each year my brothers and I celebrate both Hari Raya and Christmas with different parts of our family. Cousins, aunts and uncles have also married outside their ethnicity and faith — their spouses are mostly Chinese Christians and Indian Hindus — so the Lunar New Year and Deepavali are bustlingly active times. As an Indian-Muslim, I used to attend youth activities at, and now volunteer with, both Yayasan Mendaki and the Singapore Indian Development Association (SINDA), the respective self-help groups for the Malay/Muslim and Indian communities.

This interstitial existence, both within and among different ethnic, religious and linguistic communities, has given me more than my fair share of diversity-related stories. Once, I ordered drinks from an Indian stall owner at Newton Circus, asking in Malay for "*tek tarik dua, bandung satu*" (two *teh tarik*s and one *bandung*). The stall owner replied in Tamil and, when I said I did not speak it, asked me: "*Apa macam punya Mama, tak tahu cakap ...*" (What kind of Indian cannot speak Tamil...?), accompanied by a look of total disdain. On another occasion, I volunteered as the Master of Ceremonies at the SINDA Excellence Awards ceremony and was faced with the challenge of pronouncing the sometimes complex names of Tamil recipients. Thankfully, a very patient SINDA staff member was willing to walk me through the intricacies of what, in a poem I later wrote about the experience, I described as "rolling l's and lolling r's".

Recently, I have had slightly less disconcerting experiences as a volunteer facilitator with the Southeast Community Development Council's "Explorations into Faiths" programme. Affectionately called EIF, the programme brings people of different faith traditions (and some from no particular tradition) together to share experiences of how their beliefs are lived everyday. The programme's staples are monthly dialogues, held at a different place of worship each month, starting with a tour-cum-introduction to the host community and followed by a dialogue on a pre-chosen theme. Previous dialogues have covered a wide range of issues, including "Faith and Water", "Faith and the Mundane Life" and "Faith and International Relations".

We often hear exhortations to find unity in diversity, to manage our differences so that they do not becomes sources of conflict or, worse, violence. The stories above remind me that we do not always hear details on how this process of "management" can be carried out. This paper suggests tentative thoughts on three principles that can help individuals and societies navigate their respective diversities, encapsulated in the idea that we must all strive to be reasonable persons of goodwill.

REASON AND RATIONALITY

The idea of a reasonable person derives from a test in British Law that is applied on the basis of an intelligent non-expert (that is, reasonable) person, being put in a position to consider the evidence that might have been available at a place or time. The test involves asking the hypothetical question: what would a reasonable person do under these circumstances, given the evidence or being exposed to a particular situation? Implicit in this is the notion that reasonable persons apply logic to situations, rather than make decisions based purely on emotion or primal causalities like ethnicity or tribe. Such persons deploy rigorous arguments in support of their claims or beliefs. They accept the principle of falsifiability i.e. that any ideas, whoever their originator, can possibly be proven wrong.

Reasonable persons are central in the effective navigation of diversity because they apply vigorous scientific thinking rather than succumb to the emotional or psychic pulls of "isms" and "ologies" which, unfettered, can precipitate conflict. Acceptance of falsifiability also keeps them humble, lubricating the exchange of ideas by reducing dogmatism and doctrinaire thinking. My family background has made me instinctively aware of this idea because, as far back as I remember remembering, any ideas I had about my ethnicity or faith continually rubbed corners with those of my family members. As a child, I knew but could not always articulate how they were both similar and different from me and my brothers. I first encountered the idea of a reasonable person in fully articulated form while I was a first-year undergraduate at Oxford, listening to Amartya Sen deliver the 1998 Romanes Lecture. His lecture title elegantly captured how we need to apply "Reason before Identity" in making assessments and decisions — similar to what the philosopher René Descartes called shining "the natural light of Reason" on situations. The stories above, together with other personal experiences, have made me realise that Reason provides three key insights for situations where we interact with diverse communities.

First, each of us, while individual, is also plural, with many interacting identities of our own. This may seem counterintuitive, given that the term "diversity" is usually applied socially, referring to the dimensions that mark out particular groups from others. Such conceptions of "Us vs Them" can be based on a range of markers: gender, ethnicity, race, religion, language, nation, professional affiliation, tribe, or educational background, among others. However, a less frequently used, but equally resonant, definition of diversity applies within individuals — like me, with mixed parentage and hyphenated identities, or who balance the different aspects of their professional, personal and other identities in a dynamic equilibrium. The recent policy shift to allow double-barrelled ethnicities on Singaporean identity cards reflects the growing prevalence and awareness of such individual diversity.

Second, an individual's different identities matter more or less at different times and in different contexts. Attending a class reunion reinforces my sense of being from a particular school, being at work underscores my professional affiliations as a civil servant, going to the mosque on Hari Raya is a spiritual experience, visiting my paternal grandmother for Christmas is about spending time with family. This is not to suggest that some identities, like our ethnicity or faith, do not define us in significant and profound ways, but I would venture that their salience varies according to situation. Even as our identities interact, Reason helps us keep them conceptually distinct. A similar argument is made in Amartya Sen's *Identity and Violence* (2006); its telling subtitle intimates at how primordial identities like race and religion create "The Illusion of Destiny", whereas logic tells us that no part of our identity should be tyrannical over all others at all times, no matter how resonant and powerful it may be.

Third, Reason helps us realise that each aspect of our multiple identities can generate connections between us and many, if not all, other people. I feel this particularly strongly when interacting with family on my father's side. Growing up, my paternal grandmother told me stories from the Old Testament, emphasising how both Christians and Muslims celebrate the lives of Abraham, Moses, David, Jesus and other great Biblical figures. As I grew older, I realised that the Lord's Prayer and the Muslim *Sura Al-Fatihah*, while not identical, bear remarkable similarities. The line from the Prayer, "hallowed be Thy name, on earth as it is in heaven", for instance, is similar to the *Fatihah*'s "praise be to God, the sustainer of all known and existing worlds", while the idea of being led "not into temptation" is similar to the *Fatihah*'s plea to God to "guide us on the straight path". Recently, when one of Dad's Catholic aunts passed away, I was reminded of a further similarity, in different faiths' prayers for the dead. Muslims, many Christians and some of the Hindus in our family hold prayers on the first three days after a funeral, then on the seventh, 40th and 100th days. All this helps create a lattice of shared cultural links between groups of ostensibly different backgrounds, even if the exact forms of our rituals differ.

THE IMPORTANCE OF PERSONS

Applied alone, Reason can come across as slightly cold and clinical. It is therefore useful to temper it by recognising and valuing the person-hood in each individual. This is critical in making us reasonable persons, rather than mere automatons applying a Reason-imitating algorithm. Belief in person-hood is not a new idea. Across a range of belief systems, both faith-based and humanist, we can find an emphasis on a non-derogable core of humanity, resident in any individual, whatever the accoutrements of his/her identities and affiliations. One source of this in the liberal political tradition is clear; but it can also be justified spiritually, for example, in the belief of several faiths that there is an element of the divine in all of us, or the Muslim concept of each person occupying a special position in Creation as God's vicegerent on Earth. Belief in individual person-hood is a prerequisite for meaningful reciprocity among people, where one obeys the Golden Rule and does unto others, according them the same respect, rights, entitlements and privileges that one expects in turn.

Such belief in person-hood does not mean fetishising individual rights to such an extent that the importance of traditions or the communal good is trivialised. Rather, it helps prevent tradition and regard for the community from becoming overwhelming sources of identity, since these must be balanced against preserving the dignity of individual persons. To use the language of political theory, reasonable persons are not just "liberal" selves, but rich "communitarian" selves, complete with traditions, cultures and multiple life narratives. In turn, the recognition that every individual is a variegated being helps us recognize the common humanity in all of us, rather than over-emphasising what Michael Ignatieff calls the "narcissism of minor difference" and reducing people who are different from us to mere abstract "others".

GOODWILL AND GOOD WILL

Goodwill is important for a society to move beyond merely tolerating to celebrating its diversity. With a thin, etiolated diversity, people reluctantly put up with differences. The existence of goodwill creates progress toward a richer appreciation of those things that make us distinct. There are different conceptions of such an expanded diversity — America's "melting pot", from which the many become one; or the non-assimilationist "unity in diversity" that Singapore and others adopt — but all rely on a fundamental bedrock of goodwill among peoples. This goodwill has three important consequences.

First, it reminds us that we have no monopoly on knowledge, and can learn together what we cannot know alone. This was brought home to me very powerfully on two recent occasions. During an EIF dialogue, one participant asked a Hindu speaker if he worshipped "one or many Gods". The answer was Zen-like in its simultaneous simplicity and complexity: it does not matter whether there is one or are many Gods. What matters is that there is "only God". I was struck by that, particularly as it reminded me that any single human conception of the Divine is necessarily limited. Sometimes, the path to deeper understanding of the nuances and complexities involved can be indicated by traditions outside the ones with which we grew up. A similar experience was with a Jewish friend, who mentioned that one of the Hebrew words for God was *Elohim*, the plural of the singular *Elowah*. The etymology of the word is interesting — it originated from pre-monotheistic days and referred to the multiple gods worshipped by the predecessors of Abraham, but gradually came to apply to the "one God" of the Israelites. I find it instructive that a plural noun is now used to signify the Divine, acting in its own quiet way as a reminder that human ideas about what is single or many pale in comparison to life's larger truths.

Second, goodwill reminds us to give others the benefit of the doubt when they seem to offend us. While others have obligations not to cause offence in speech and action, each of us also has the prerogative not to take offence. Apparently racist remarks often stem from ignorance rather than malice, and being bigger persons helps us both to understand and address such situations with information, rather than indignation.

The natural consequence of realising we have no monopoly on truth and have a prerogative not to take offence leads to the third benefit of goodwill: it helps us deal with sensitive issues by building trust and accommodating differences. Attitudes of goodwill could, for instance, have helped defuse some of the tension over whether McDonald's should have retained the pig figurine in its Lunar New Year toy line-up; just as some tense situations where HDB void decks have been double-booked, for Malay weddings and Chinese funerals, have been defused with a little give-and-take.

IDEALS, PRAGMATISM AND POLICY

Being reasonable persons of goodwill helps us navigate the choppy and sometimes-uncharted waters of diversity, but it is not a panacea. Reason is neither uniformly nor universally distributed in most societies, so it requires careful nurturing through education and exposure, rather than being left to chance. Even where it is widespread, Reason also has limits, at which points powerful emotions start to come into play. I suspect this is one reason why interfaith marriages, while more numerous than before, still face so many obstacles today. Rising above these challenges requires not just vision, but also healthy realism. It will help if we view the navigation of diversity as a journey — where we are all, in the words of a friend of mine who is a Catholic priest, "fellow pilgrims" — rather than a final destination. To be translated into public policy, diversity-promoting measures will need to create space for dreams and aspirational goals, rather than fixate purely on what is achievable in the immediate or short-term. Emphasising the process and journey involved will also call for a mindset change and acceptance of success metrics that may not necessarily translate directly into easily concretised performance indicators. In addition, focusing on being reasonable *persons* of goodwill means supplementing (not supplanting) our current scepticism about the role(s) individuals can play in society, while also exercising sufficient caution about possibly creating cults of personality.

CONCLUDING THOUGHTS

Nations can base their organisation on ethnic nationalism, centred on common primordial ancestries like ethnicity or language; or rally around civic nationalism, which emphasises common values and attitudes. For a multicultural state like Singapore, reasonable persons of goodwill can provide a resilient base for the broader structures of a civic nation. In so doing, they also build a foundation for a robust deliberative democracy where voices are enabled, where the linguistic and experiential reference points required for coherent common narratives can be found and where legitimate different perspectives are accommodated and celebrated.

III

One Gracious Society

Considerable efforts to foster a greater sense of civic mindedness through the years underscore the importance of graciousness in Singaporean society. Does a mere understanding of differences lead to the maintenance and development of Singapore's cultural and social resilience? How can we have more "Heart" and bond with each other without a top-down prescription? Are we managing the problems of the different segments of the population and their needs? Graciousness is not just about our daily social interactions; it is also about being aware of how our lifestyles impact the common environment we inhabit. Do Singaporeans care about healthy living and sustainable development? This panel will focus on these issues and consider the scope for more "heartware" in an increasingly competitive society.

CHAPTER 5

One Gracious Society

PAULIN TAY STRAUGHAN

I felt that this session is perhaps one of the most exciting sessions because the notion of being "gracious" has caught the attention of headlines. Just today, we were informed by *The Straits Times* that we are a dirty city because the beaches are littered. If not for the very very hardworking pool of labourers, we would probably be living in a very dirty country. This panel is going to engage you in a discourse on graciousness. Graciousness is, from a sociological perspective, an abstract construct because it is one of those mental imageries where, when we invoke the term, everybody immediately knows or seems to know what we are talking about. However, when it comes to concrete operationalisation, we defer. So perhaps that is one reason why the notion of graciousness is so elusive.

What does graciousness entail? What does it mean and, more importantly, who gets to define what describes graciousness? When we think of graciousness, immediately we think about the Kindness Movement, we think about the courtesy campaigns. So we tend to think and restrict our thoughts to graciousness exchanged on an individual-to-individual level. But there is a more complex concept than that.

Graciousness can also be conceptualised as exchange between individuals and groups, or between groups and groups. For example, the relationship between the haves and the have-nots, between citizens and immigrants and, at an even higher level, between the state and society. The underlying thread here then is, if we ask ourselves, "Are we a gracious society?" Would there be a consensus on where our achievements are at this point?

And if there is some mumbling from the ground that we have a long way more to go, then the next important question would be, "Whose responsibility is it to ensure that Singapore is a gracious society?" Is it the responsibility of families as primary caregivers of children, or is it the responsibility of schools to inculcate the right norms and values in our kids? Or is it the responsibility of the government to ensure that Singapore is able to achieve a passing grade on this very important social indicator?

This afternoon, my distinguished panel will attempt to answer some of these questions.

CHAPTER 6

In Search of Graciousness

TERENCE CHONG

INTRODUCTION: A JOURNEY TOWARDS NATIONHOOD

Singapore has always been in search of graciousness. Right from the early years after independence to the present day, the search for graciousness has never been far from political discourse. And although the term is a relatively new addition to our public civil vocabulary, the idea and desire for a Singapore society that is spiritually and culturally elevated from the everyday coarseness of working life have preoccupied the minds of our political leaders right from the start. This chapter takes a historical perspective of the country's search for graciousness and strives to make three points. Firstly, this search must be seen as part and parcel of the People's Action Party (PAP) government's understanding of Singapore society as something to be perpetually shaped, polished and upgraded according to specific visions of the day. Secondly, it has been largely propelled by an economic agenda or instrumentalist rationale and, thirdly, it has shifted, over the years, from one of national consciousness towards that of a global city that has to welcome foreign talent and integrate new citizens.

Singapore's search for "graciousness" has come in various guises and encouraged by different policies. And this search is a Sisyphean task that will never end, not because there is something in the Singaporean DNA that is allergic to civility or consideration for others, but because it is a purposefully vague concept that is intimately tied up with our nation-building project. The ongoing search for graciousness is part of the never-ending journey towards nationhood. Like big abstract concepts such as "multiculturalism", "social integration" and "equality", there are no clear and authoritative markers of "graciousness" to inform us of where we stand and how far more we need to go to achieve it. Or as then-Prime Minister Lee Kuan Yew put it, courtesy "is a marathon with no finishing line".

It is this vagueness and ambiguity that have proven to be so useful when it comes to shaping society. According to George Yeo, then-Minister for Information and the Arts, "The Courtesy Campaign helps us to build a Singapore nation. We inherited from the British a Singapore that prospered as a trading post but had no sense of nationhood. With independence, our goal must be to create a sense of oneness among the diverse groups that live here. Part of the glue is proper behaviour which courtesy expresses [...] While our strategic objective to promote courtesy is fixed, our tactics must constantly be refreshed". (Terence Lee, 2002). As noted by scholars elsewhere, "the discourse of courtesy is arguably one of the many tools created to define the scope of citizenship, identity and nationhood in Singapore" (Terence Lee, 2002). By pointing to a distant but easily understood notion of "graciousness", one is able to outline broad visions of society that celebrates dominant interests and orthodoxy. For example, by strictly confining the meaning of "graciousness" to notions of civility, social etiquette and social and cultural tolerance towards each other, instead of broadening its definition to include political graciousness or tolerance for alternative politics, we are in fact championing and celebrating specific interests and orthodox ideas. It is this taken-for-grantedness of big concepts that makes it so useful for shaping society's values and interests. And it is precisely our desire to create a new Singapore society that our life-long search for "graciousness" began.

CREATING A "CIVILISED" AND "CULTURED" SOCIETY WITH THE ARTS

Singapore's separation from Malaysia in 1965 made it necessary for the Old Guard leaders to envisage a "new Singapore" — a society that was distinct from Malaysia, one that would give Singaporeans a unique identity and national culture that would galvanise citizens for the uncertain paths ahead. Whether it was multiculturalism, meritocracy or the campaign to create a "rugged society", as it was in 1966, or a "clean and green society" in the

1970s, the national project was to establish as quickly as possible a shared national identity that different ethnic groups could relate to. This new Singaporean society would, first, in the minds of the young PAP government, be imagined as a *tabula rasa*, free from the ideologies and values of a Malay-privileging Malaysia; and second, must be willing to "adopt a new set of attitudes, a new set of values, a new set of perspectives" that were perceived to be necessary for survival, or what Chan Heng Chee, in her book *The Politics of Survival 1965–1967*, termed the "ideology of survival".

Long before there was any "graciousness" campaign, there was the campaign to promote the arts. According to Oscar Wilde, "It is through Art, and through Art only, that we can realise our perfection; through Art and Art only that we can shield ourselves from the sordid perils of actual existence." It is unlikely that Wilde was prerequisite bedtime reading for the PAP ruling elite but it certainly shared the playwright's romantic ideas on Art. For one, the PAP government saw traditional and mainstream forms of art such as painting, sculpture, literature or drama primarily as a means to ennoble the soul and to create a society that was civilised and cultured. For the ruling elite, the dichotomy between high culture and other forms of "lower" popular cultural expressions was clear and unproblematic. "Good art" was a vehicle for the very best that culture had to offer, defined most famously by Matthew Arnold in 1869 as the "pursuit of our total perfection" and "the best which has been thought and said in the world". And it was through the consumption of good or high art that Singaporeans could become "civilised" and "cultured".

Indeed, as early as 1964, there were government perceptions that people in Malaya, especially Singapore, lacked the finer graces. Yusof Ishak, later to become Singapore's first President, noted that:

> For it used to be a common slander in the old days, that while the people of Malaysia, and in particular Singapore, that we're good at making money, they're indifferent to the finer graces of civilised life.

Such government perceptions of Singaporeans lacking social graces and refinement have persisted till today with then-Prime Minister Goh Chok Tong warning against becoming a *"parvenu* society". Taking up Yusof Ishak's theme was S. Rajaratnam who, speaking at the opening of a Balinese exhibition at the Institute of Southeast Asian Studies on 28 December 1971, mused that:

> Music, painting, drama, literature and a concern for beauty generally are what transforms a prosperous society into a civilised society. Without these Singapore remains not more than a prosperous and efficiently run *pasar malam.*

Other PAP leaders followed suit with the Senior Minister of State for Foreign Affairs Encik Rahim Ishak, while officiating over a Chinese painting exhibition on 6 Dec 1977, opining that:

> Art generally can help make our domestic lives that much more pleasant and agreeable. Some of us become embarrassed when we are called "ugly Singaporeans.

Art was used by the PAP government with a Victorian instrumentalism where moral aesthetics and the quest for truth, through the production and consumption of high art, would lead to a more enlightened and cultured society. These government discourses should be seen as the state's attempt to mould an ideal society. On the one hand, Singaporeans were reminded to work harder, to stay ahead of the competition and be wary of the disastrous consequences of falling behind other countries. On the other, they were exhorted to be more refined, appreciative of the arts, cultured and gracious. All these represented the government's project to perpetually mould and shape an ideal citizenry that would withstand the challenges and demands of globalisation — a project that persists today.

THE NATIONAL COURTESY CAMPAIGN

The National Courtesy Campaign, launched in June 1979, is probably the most recognisable and iconic symbol of the top-down approach towards instilling "graciousness". Initiated under the Ministry of Culture and helmed by the Singapore Courtesy Council, the campaign, more than most, married notions of "graciousness" with a strong instrumentalist social rationale. This can be seen in the string of courtesy campaigns in the run-up to the National Courtesy Campaign launched in 1979. Before the 1979 National Courtesy Campaign, there were the Bus Safety and Courtesy

Campaign (1968); National "Safety First" Council Road Courtesy Campaigns (1972–1973); and the Safety and Courtesy Campaign Week (1972–1973). These were essentially road safety campaigns that leveraged on ideas of courtesy and graciousness to get their message across. The aim of these campaigns was, of course, to reduce road accidents and to facilitate speedier transportation networks.

Perhaps the most obviously instrumentalist use of the Courtesy Campaign was in its first incarnation at the hands of the then-Singapore Tourist Promotion Board (STPB) in 1978. The objective of the STPB-driven campaign was not to get Singaporeans to be courteous to each other but to tourists and foreigners in order that they might form a good impression of the country. The campaign focused on promoting courtesy among staff in the hospitality and transport industries. Front-line staff — hotel managers, chambermaids, porters, drivers, and waitresses — were taught the importance of courtesy and friendliness towards their guests and customers. Taxi drivers and civil servants were educated on the finer points of courtesy through training films while the Retail Merchants Association (RMA) conducted role-playing scenarios of courteous and discourteous acts to bring home the message to its staff. (Singapore Courtesy Council, 1999) The aim to be polite only to tourists prompted then-Prime Minister Lee Kuan Yew to re-launch the STPB campaign as a National Campaign in 1979. At the launch of the National Courtesy Campaign at the Singapore Conference Hall on 1 June, 1979, PM Lee noted:

> Last year the Tourist Promotion Board launched a courtesy campaign to make Singaporeans more polite to tourists. I followed the campaign with interest and amusement: interest because most people were responsive to the campaign; amusement because no one protested that it was absurd to teach Singaporeans to be polite only to tourists. This National Courtesy Campaign is at my prodding.

Although the National Courtesy Campaign was re-launched by PM Lee with a stronger focus on Singaporeans, it did not lose any of its instrumentalist agendum, such as transport efficiency or social harmony. In March 2001, the campaign was taken over by the Singapore Kindness Movement. The National Courtesy Campaign did not emerge in an

Source: National Archives of Singapore (1979)

Figure 1 National Courtesy Campaign Poster, 1979

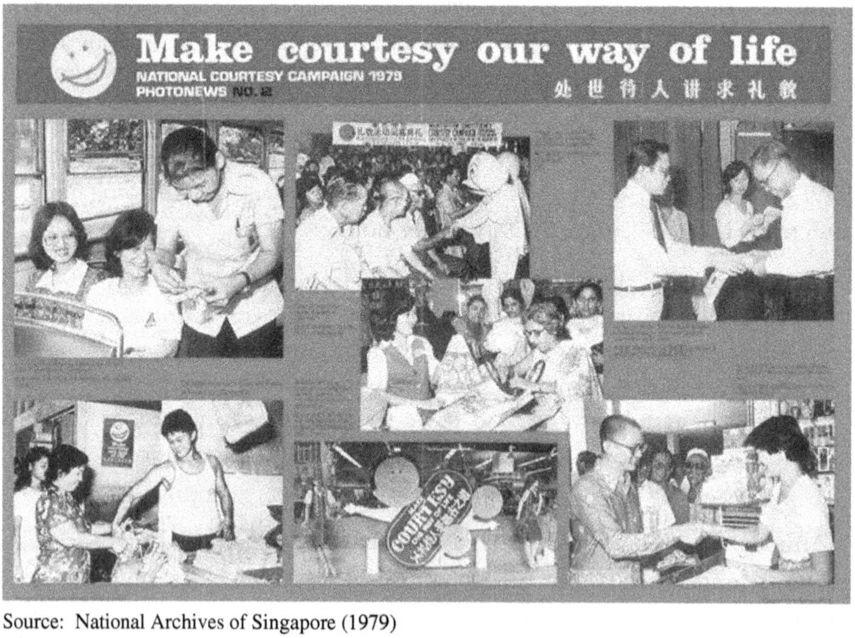

Source: National Archives of Singapore (1979)

Figure 2 National Courtesy Campaign 1979 Poster: "Make courtesy our way of life"

ideological vacuum. It came at a time when the PAP government felt that Singaporeans were in danger of becoming "deculturalised". The decade of high economic growth had been manifested through the influx of mass consumer goods and popular culture from the West, much of which were gleefully consumed by Singaporeans who were enjoying higher levels of disposable income by the late 1970s and early 1980s. Conspicuous consumption and the ubiquity of popular culture gave rise to government concerns that many Singaporeans were becoming too "Westernised" or "individualistic" — leading to two seminal government reports that were released in 1978 and 1979.

The first was the *Report on the Ministry of Education* by Dr Goh Keng Swee, followed by the *Report on Moral Education*, submitted by the late Ong Teng Cheong. Both reports expressed the need for greater moral and civics guidance in schools. Both noted that students and teachers were not taking the existing Civics and Education for Living programme seriously because it was a non-examinable subject. Meanwhile the *Report on Moral Education* recommended the teaching of religious studies in schools because they were better transmitters of moral values. This resulted in the implementation of Religious Studies in 1984 whereby major religions — Christianity, Islam, Buddhism and Hinduism — together with Confucian ethics, were taught in secondary schools. In announcing the policy, Dr Goh Keng Swee warned that Singapore needed to avoid the "decline in moral standards" taking place in the West.

There is little doubt that the political elite, together with large segments of the conservative society, felt that the country was undergoing a profound moral crisis. Such moral crises often exude the spectre of cultural loss and the demise of tradition, accompanied by the existential fear that one's way of life and identity is coming to an end, giving way to cultural and political forces that are new, alien and unwelcome. The promotion of religious teachings in schools and the National Courtesy Campaign were useful in that they signalled a return to the way things were, where good old-fashioned values and civility were celebrated, thus offering comfort and security to those who were unsettled and alienated by the capricious stream of modernity and capitalism.

Perhaps more importantly, such campaigns and policy initiatives demonstrate the PAP government's pre-emptive attitudes and its long reach into the social and cultural lives of its citizens. Without waiting for counter-movements or sub-cultures from the grassroots to develop in resistance to conspicuous consumption, hyper-capitalism or the sense of anomie that usually accompanies modernity and urbanisation, the result of which might have been socio-political enclaves and greater political disaffection, the PAP government's use of courtesy campaigns, the promotion of the arts and ethnic culture effectively stemmed any possibility of aggressive reaction to neo-capitalism and modernity, while ensuring that such grassroots unease would be addressed by state-sponsored campaigns. In sum, the search for graciousness not only allowed society to be shaped with the values believed by the ruling elite to be necessary to meet the challenges of globalisation, but it also served as a useful salve for the side-effects from the country's relentless drive for economic growth and development.

CONCLUSION: FROM NATIONAL TO GLOBAL CONSCIOUSNESS?

The campaigns of the past had an undeniable role in the nation-building process. Collectively, they paint a vivid picture of how leaders imagined society and perceived its flaws, as well as how to remedy them. They were prescriptions for a better society. There is no doubt that the campaigns for a "rugged society", a "clean and green" society, and a more courteous Singapore have contributed to greater self-consciousness. What all these different campaigns had in common was the underlying aim to nurture some sense of national consciousness. Whether or not they were instrumentalist in nature, the intended subjects of such campaigns were Singaporeans themselves (the ill-fated STPB campaign aside). Whether or not these campaigns were designed with the initial objective of increasing productivity, transportation efficiency or social harmony, they were highly successful in providing Singaporeans with the conceptual vocabulary to think of each other as shared stakeholders of this tiny island-state. Given the multiple cleavages of ethnicity, religion and language, Singaporeans were confronted with the realisation that, though different, they all had ownership over this land, and were encouraged to widen common spaces through courteous acts.

But that was then. Today as both a nation *and* a global city we often have to juggle conflicting demands. The global city, on one hand, demands the all-out attraction of foreign talent, while the nation is anxious that these newcomers do not displace citizens. Even as the global city must be a node in the global matrix, the nation finds it necessary to embrace certain global trends while rejecting others. The broader and profound question Singaporeans have to ask themselves in the coming years is which form of existence will ensure their survival — nation or global city? The answer to which determines the priority with which we accord, not just campaigns, but also the way we perceive each other. We now have a population of 5 million. Only 3.2 million are Singapore citizens — 500,000 are PRs and 1.3 million are foreigners. Have the objectives of "graciousness" campaigns shifted their focus from creating a sense of shared identity towards the integration of foreigners? Has the instrumentalist rationale behind "graciousness" campaigns returned to the old STPB campaign to make "foreigners" feel welcome? Or do we need to expand our current definitions of "graciousness" and not lose sight of the ongoing nation-building project?

REFERENCES

Arnold, Matthew. 2008 [1869]. *Culture and Anarchy: An Essay in Political and Social Criticism*, p. 5. Middlesex: The Echo Library.

Chan, Heng Chee (1971). *The Politics of Survival 1965–1967*, p. 49. Singapore and Kuala Lumpur: Oxford University Press.

Singapore Courtesy Council (1999). *Courtesy — More than a Smile*, p. 21, 113. Singapore: Ministry of Information and the Arts.

Lee, Terence (2002). The Politics of Civil Society in Singapore. *Asian Studies Review*, Vol. 26, No. 1, pp. 97–117.

Tan, Jason (2000). The Politics of Religious Knowledge in Singapore Secondary Schools. In *Curriculum Politics, Policy, Practice: Cases in Comparative Context*, Catherine Cornbleth (ed.), p. 82. New York: State University of New York Press.

Wilde, Oscar (1997). *The Critic as Artist*. California: Green Integer.

7

Living Graciously in Singapore

BRAEMA MATHIAPARANAM

I would like to first try and define graciousness, even though it is not so easy to find clear definitions. Interestingly, the concept of graciousness has also undergone some metamorphosis. According to the *Merriam-Webster English Dictionary*, the Middle English concept of graciousness in the 14th century was akin to "godliness" in an era of feudalism and Christian influence. Embodied in that concept was also a notion "to please", coming from a place of obedience to God and to Lords. Today graciousness has evolved to connote kindness, courtesy, charm, good taste, generosity of spirit, tact and actions that denote being merciful and compassionate. Other Web searches on graciousness also reveal similar concepts. As such, there is a refrain to the concept with characteristics that signify warmth, courtesy compassion and charm.

Nevertheless it is not enough to say that each of these attributes can be applied or understood without further discussion to identify the tenets of each characteristic. For example, what does being charming mean amongst the diverse cultures in one country? To the Chinese, it is charming to make slurping noises when drinking soup but to many English it is unbecoming behaviour. It is uncouth if you eat noisily in an English home and equally unbecoming if you eat quietly in a Chinese home. As such, it is important to realise that each attribute of graciousness has its own field of meaning and a cultural context in which it operates.

For the purpose of this essay, I will limit the concept of graciousness to compassion and courteous behaviour, operating in a context of universal values of being caring and thoughtful towards each other.

In Singapore's early history of colonisation and the heady post-independent days, there were community care services initiated by people to help those who were less fortunate. Some of these initiatives include the setting up of what is now known as the Singapore Council of Women's Organisations, the Asian Welfare Women's Association and the Singapore Cheshire Home. In addition, there are many visible legacies today of individual acts of kindness and justice — Chinese adult women in their 60s today who had been cared for by Malay and Indian families when they were put up for adoption. Clan associations — the precursor of the present self-help groups — were also formed with the primary purpose of pooling money and resources. Places of worship were built and traditional rituals were also performed as communities came together to make them happen. We also saw philanthropy through the generosity of patriarchs such as Mr Tan Tock Seng, Mr Tan Kah Kee and Mr Lee Seng Gee, who set up foundations or built institutions for the poor.

In terms of charm and courtesy, there was an openness that has been described as having the *gotong royong* and *kongsi*. Both words — the former a Malay word and the latter a Hokkien word — mean community spiritedness of shared responsibilities. In fact some examples are documented in the work of National University of Singapore lecturer Dr Brenda Yeoh whose thesis is a report on how the early migrant communities worked to share their space (beds, even) and meals and also stood up against any intrusion by the colonial masters who at one point wanted to claim the pavement space — which was used as sleeping quarters — to widen the road.

As we went into the nation-building phase, with the ruling party taking over much of the decision-making and implementation for the betterment of the people of Singapore, it is my view that much of this early community-spiritedness gave way to an economic pragmatism. This meant that most people were focused on singular economic pursuits, like access to shelter, clean water, food, good schools, the best tertiary education. As the government asserted its role as an inclusive provider for all who needed help, it became easier to step back from being responsible for the community. It became easier to pass on the role of minding society to the government with the people feeling less empowered to engage in the process as the government took on a domineering role.

It was also easier to become more comfortable with giving money and time to help out at agencies that provided direct services. This meant that it was easier to be an armchair giver through donations while watching television, than to get engaged in upstream measures such as picking up on more advocacy-related causes. This emphasis on direct services, in my view, highlights how the graciousness concept of being compassionate and kind, seems to fall short of recognising that dignity is also equally important. In fact, in working harder to ask for permanent solutions to improve the condition of people and with a view to empowering them, it means that we are being gracious to ask that the imbalance be resolved with access to opportunities rather than through welfare.

One example of how welfare has reigned over advocacy is the case of people with disabilities. They still have limited access to facilities as, even after 44 years of nationhood, not all of our public transport can accommodate those in wheelchairs. The few advocates are seen as disruptive whilst those who provide services for the community are seen as being compassionate. But community service organisations (CSOs) that advocate empowerment and independence of the disabled person are playing a role in building up a gracious society as they are asking for upstream solutions without compromising the dignity of the disabled person.

Even organisations that work towards enhancing the well-being of people are often seen as charities and voluntary welfare organisations (VWO). Some began as citizen initiatives and remain entrenched in providing direct services, stepping back from upstream measures that are often advocacy-oriented. It is also equally important to assess how we serve one another. If we are truly a gracious people, how we serve one another must come from a place of observing and preserving the dignity of other individuals in society. If we refer to the people whom we serve as beneficiaries, it also begs the question of how we perceive them. Where is the graciousness when such terminology implies an inequality between those who provide and those who receive?

If we were to look at the private sector, there is a disconnect in how companies respond to observing corporate social responsibility (CSR). It has come to mean big donations for charitable causes, which is all good. But CSR is also about a code of conduct which includes how personnel treat each other within a company, for example: how colleagues are treated and whether they have rights to flexible work arrangements and fair trade practices. If a company treats differently a woman who is pregnant or a woman wearing a headscarf, that company is discriminating and cannot be CSR-oriented. CSR is about dignity and being gracious. CSR is an attribute of being gracious, being mindful of people, being compassionate. It has also to be internalised within the company and become part of employment guidelines.

The government too plays a role in this discussion of graciousness as it sends signals to the population on what ought to be done through its campaigns and its appointed persons of goodwill who champion causes, But sometimes, government leaders and spokesmen also dabble in doublespeak. Since 2004, when the Prime Minister gave his speech at the Harvard Club about working towards a more open society, the government has sent out a series of mixed signals on how open one can be. One important aspect of an open society is to engage in dialogue, a two-way process that gives equal respect to both parties, even if both were to disagree on the common points. Have we reached this level of maturity and graciousness where we can sit across a table and have differing points of views on a common subject matter and know how to part from the table without feeling that there is a traitor in the room just because the views are different?

It may be a bit odd to talk about graciousness from such a perspective of dealing with diverse views. But what is graciousness? It is courtesy. It is giving respect to diverse views and learning to deal with the diversity. Recently, Senior Minister Goh Chok Tong made a gracious comment on opposition parties attracting better educated people. This was a gracious comment as it showed that we can deal with such a spread of well-qualified people across political parties. It is good for the whole of Singapore as it embraces openness and a graciousness to let the competition sort itself out through the ballot box. This, hopefully, marks the beginning of a process to deal with electioneering and candidates from the various political parties without compromising on being gracious even when the stakes are high.

We can no longer run the risk of having episodic graciousness movements or campaigns. We need instead to promote a process that instils values, minimises doublespeak and leads by example. Campaigns are also difficult to measure. How effective have our campaigns been if people still litter when no one is watching or if cyclists and motorists squabble over use of road space? Some less-than-charming habits include: letting a door slam into a person's face instead of holding it open for him or her, not signalling while driving, reserving seats at public eating places like hawker centres, and asking for the cheapest prices without a care for the cultural handiwork of the people or fair trade practices. It ought to embarrass us that our forefathers may have had better graciousness in knowing how to give space, respect and dignity to various users in that common space.

HOW TO EMBRACE GRACIOUSNESS

So how do we really embrace the notions of graciousness from the definition that I have worked on — being compassionate and courteous?

Firstly, it has to come from a place of instilling values. I went to Canossian Convent Primary School. What I have taken away from Canossian Convent are the constant lessons in ethics where morals were taught through down-to-earth examples, like how not to let a door slam into another person's face. At home, values were also reinforced and there was little room for a disconnect. If we really want to start shifting gears and work towards becoming more gracious, we have to embrace the indicators that show us to be gracious and get that value system across to our children in as consistent a manner as possible.

Secondly, topics that provoke thinking and critical analysis need to be introduced from a young age into the school for children so that they can deal with diverse views. It cannot all be held back till the General Paper stage or only introduced into certain schools. I would also say that Literature should be re-introduced to all classes as a non-examinable subject. Literature deals with multiculturalism. It deals with people, passions, emotions, discouragement: the whole gamut of experiences a human being goes through. It is an important humanities subject that gives us our humanity. It also gives teachers many opportunities to deal with a diversity of views as well as value systems within societies.

Thirdly, I do believe that laws are important. Laws give a signal to society as to what we value most. That the Compulsory Education Act still does not include children with disabilities signals, as a nation, our lack of graciousness — we do not believe that these children are important enough. We are also saying that such children deserve our goodwill, but not their place as equals in our society. When the right laws are introduced to preserve and protect the dignity of all members of a society, it is a signal of the proper value system. A country with anti-discrimination laws recognises human failings and strives to put things right for others who have been victimised.

Fourthly, we also need to distinguish between living graciously and gracious living. Currently there is much marketing of gracious living — waterfront living, elegant homes, beautiful parks, underground pools, etc. But we also need to work towards living graciously in gracious-living surroundings. But they cannot be replacements for each other as these are two different concepts. One can spit in the pool in gracious surroundings but living there with care and dignity for the others, means blowing the whistle on such recalcitrant behaviour. When we can have both, Singapore would have truly arrived.

Lastly, the narrative on graciousness needs dedication and consistency. From time to time, it is resurrected in various campaigns. I would like to suggest not a campaign but, perhaps with the help of the media and other stakeholders in our society, to run a remedial effort to instil one good habit per year. For example, we could try to change one micro social bad habit, such as not holding open the door for the person behind. In five years, we would have attempted changing five bad social habits. I know it can be controlling but steering is always hard work.

I would like to end with a quote from Martin Luther King which speaks of the essence of graciousness. "Everybody can be great because anybody can serve. You don't have to have a college degree to serve. You don't have to make your subject and verb agree to serve. You only need a heart, full of grace, and a soul generated by love for the other person."

CHAPTER 8

Kiasu Monkeys and Chicken Pies

GAN SU-LIN

DISAPPOINTMENT, DILEMMA, DECISION

Bewilderment, dismay, tears. These were the three regular features of my first year living in Singapore after having spent 11 years in the United States.

It was June 1996 and I was a newly minted PhD with a specialisation in media psychology and a dissertation on factors contributing to the palliative potential of entertainment. Unlike most Singaporeans — and for reasons quite irrelevant to this presentation — I shied away from the big cities and spent 11 years studying and working in Louisiana and Alabama. They were wonderful years spent immersed in Southern hospitality and civility, and I only rarely encountered the racism which many Singaporeans seem to think runs rampant in the Southern US.

I loved the South. Strangers would smile and say "Hi" or "good morning" to each other, customers said "thank you" to the check-out cashier at the grocery store, people addressed each other as "Sir" and "Ma'am", they stopped and waited for you to respond to "how you doin' today?" and — my favourite — neighbours would bring a chicken pie or other edibles when you returned from out of town because "I figured you'd be tired from all that driving. Here's supper so you don't have to worry about cooking."

Within months of arriving in Singapore, I had decided I hated this place where my overwhelming experience was with people who did not care about each other, where "excuse me" was a challenge rather than a request, where my cheery "good morning!" was returned with looks of either fear or suspicion, where it was normal at service counters to hear "I want ..." rather than "may I please ...", and where even schoolchildren felt it was all right to litter because "the cleaners need the job *mah*!"

My presentation offers you a very personal look at one Singaporean's experience with the good, the bad, and the ugly of Singaporean youths and offers one person's observations on the reasons we are not a more gracious people. We will also peek into the bases for the optimism and idealism that have kept this Singaporean rooted to her homeland even though there's still much that she doesn't like about it.

EDUCATED, OR MERELY LITERATE AND NUMERATE?

As I became increasingly disenchanted with being in Singapore, I found myself with a growing list of things that, for me, exemplified the ugliness and horror of this place which I thought could be my home.

I was teaching at the university and it shocked me that supposedly educated young people would:

- Walk through a door that I was holding open for a visitor or older person, and without so much as a 'thank you' or a smile
- Block passageways and stairwells to engage in conversation, utterly oblivious to the people trying to get past from either side
- Engage in loud conversations in public spaces, including bellowing into their mobile phones on public transport
- "Chope" extra seats on the bus or in the canteen or at the library so their bags would not have to be placed on the floor

And, ironically, I observed that these errant youths had the cheek to glare at or make snide remarks about similar discourteous behaviour from other youths!

It was toward the end of my first year in Singapore that I was horrified to realise I had been passing judgment on the young people with whom I worked. I would selectively seize upon exemplars that supported my mental conception of an ugly, miserable Singapore without sparing much thought for alternative and plausible interpretations. My exemplars had warped my construction of reality and I had turned myself into the same ugly Singaporean I thought I saw all around me.

This realisation got me wondering whether Singaporean youths were really as ungracious as I thought them to be. This, then, was the genesis of my still ongoing search for what graciousness means, why we are the way we are here in Singapore, and what we can try to do to be a nicer people.

LOOKING AT THE WORLD WITH DIFFERENT LENSES

According to the Singapore Department of Statistics, in 1993, 41.2% of Singaporeans had completed secondary education or higher. By 2003, that had become 54% and, by 2008, 89.6%. Over 15 years, there had been a 217% increase. In 1993, the literacy rate was 90.1% and in 2008, it was 96%. In 2008, the average Singaporean had completed 9.7 years of formal schooling.

Singapore youths are apparently intelligent enough to have bumped up the nation's educational achievement statistics. Yet, most have not shown me that they are civilised or couth enough to be properly considered educated.

I had a hard time reconciling the steadily increasing percentage of globe-trotting Singaporeans with higher and more formal schooling, with my own observations and anecdotal evidence from others of youths who were becoming more self-centred, selfish, and *bo chap*.

In trying to understand this paradox, I reflected on the lenses with which I viewed the world around me. Like the two faces of a coin, almost everything that happens in our lives can be positive or negative depending on the perspective we take to interpret that experience.

I offer you, here, three pairs of lenses with which to reflect on the attitudes and behaviours of our youths (or adults for that matter). I will discuss these lenses in the following contextual frame drawn from an experience involving students in my social psychology class.

I asked my students whether they would yield their seat on the train to a senior citizen. Half the class raised their hands in affirmation, while the other half looked around at each other or looked sheepish. I then asked: You offer your seat to the old lady and instead of taking that seat, she starts to berate you and to accuse you of being disrespectful of older people in believing that they cannot manage without assistance. Having had that experience, how many of you would yield your seat to another senior citizen? No more than a dozen hands went up. And, when I asked: If you see that same old lady, would you again try to offer her your seat? I saw no hands at all, although I did hear a somewhat indignant "*siao arh?*" which is the local vernacular for "Are you mad?"

- *Lack of Awareness v. Lack of Respect for Others*

The first pair of lenses asks whether or not youths are lacking in awareness of what is happening around them, or are they lacking in respect for others.

I have presented the scenario of the old lady on the MRT in many of the character and leadership development programmes to which I have contributed over the last dozen years. The resultant discussions helped me realise many youths have not learned about perspective taking and, even if they had, that learning seemed to be mostly an academic exercise.

The lack of awareness I have observed comes in two types. The first is the more obvious lack of spatial or environmental awareness. Stand outside any school at dismissal and you'll see streams of students filling the sidewalks like migrating lemmings. They are all heading in the same direction, walking abreast of each other and not making way for folk headed in the opposite direction. I have been among these unfortunate folk having to step off the sidewalk to trot along on the grass verge or on the street itself. My experience in Louisiana was that there is an imaginary line on the sidewalk and that same imaginary line is in the grocery store aisles, on the staircases, and more. People of all ages treated such spaces the same way drivers stayed in their lane!

The second type of a lack of awareness occurs at a cognitive level. The example of the old lady on the MRT demonstrated to me that youths need to and should be taught perspective-taking. My students were surprised that I asked them to offer reasons why the old lady responded to courtesy with crankiness, to imagine what it must be like to go from hale to frail, and from having others depend on you to becoming more dependent on assistance from others. My students' reactions told me they had neglected to consider that other people, like themselves, could have a bad day that gave them cause to snap and bark. And, that this one bad day did not automatically make them horrible people undeserving of common courtesy from others.

The other lens in this pair is the lack of respect for others. Just as apparently self-centred behaviour can stem from a genuine lack of awareness of how our actions or inactions are affecting others, it is also possible for ungracious behaviour to stem from a wilful disregard for and disrespect for others. This other lens is best illustrated by this retort I heard from a teenager who had been asked to give up his MRT seat to a senior citizen. He said: Why should I? I also paid my fare.

- *Diffusion of Responsibility v. Disempowerment*

Now, set awareness and lack of respect aside. Take it that a need has been noticed. Why then might help not be offered? My work with youths offered me a second pair of lenses, being, diffusion of responsibility and disempowerment.

Consider again the old lady on the MRT. You see young people not yielding their MRT seat to a senior citizen and you think "How rude of them. They should be told off." You think the thought, but do you verbalise that thought? From my observations, most Singaporeans would think but would not speak. When I inquired, the reason for not verbalising is often that someone else will surely speak up. This same reason is also what youth have given me for not responding to needs they may encounter.

The contrasting lens is that of disempowerment. Sometimes we see the need but we feel incapable of responding appropriately. I admit I am decidedly monolingual. I used to shrug apologetically and shake my head when anyone spoke to me in Mandarin. I would get as far as the "请问 …" and then I would be lost. Stupidly, it took me a while to realise that rendering assistance really was quite independent of my language limitations. I do not turn away anymore. I still shake my head and look apologetic but I put my hand up, say "Wait" and then grab anyone passing by who looks like they might speak Mandarin and sweetly ask them to interpret for me. Believe me, it has worked for me and I think it is all in the way one makes the request which starts with "Excuse me, would you help me, please?"

I have expended a lot of effort trying to get youths to realise that the combination of perceived disempowerment and diffusion of responsibility are barriers to building a cohesive, caring community. More important, I have been getting them to realise that solutions are never really far from their reach. I am glad to report at least some of my students have learned that when we do not have the skills to directly address a particular need, even a smile of encouragement or a steady hand to hold while waiting for trained aid to arrive is still meaningful help and certainly counts as an act of kindness and graciousness.

- *Approval Seeking v. Embarrassment Avoidance*

The third pair of lenses contrasts approval seeking with embarrassment avoidance. Diffusion of responsibility sometimes can be fuelled by our need to 'save face' and to avoid embarrassment. Note the example I gave earlier of folk not wanting to rebuke another for failing to yield a seat to a senior citizen. This "embarrassment avoidance" I find the most detrimental to our realisation of a gracious Singapore. It is also the cause of ungraciousness that I find the most difficult to comprehend. I am simply not able to understand how doing the right thing can be sacrificed for the sake of saving face. Is it not more detrimental to one's face to ignore someone in need? Is it not worse to look unfeeling and selfish as opposed to potentially foolish?

The alternative lens in this pair is just as troubling. I have observed many youths who choose what to do or not to do based on what they get in return. Signing up for 'flag day' or beach clean-up to earn community involvement hours, agreeing to attend particular workshops or talks because "it looks good on the resume". Even adults do this. Most of us can easily recall someone who committed hours upon hours of service in a primary school in the hopes of getting a better chance of entry for their child? I am in no way disdainful of the pursuit of benefits and personal gain but if these are the primary and, worse, sole, reason for engaging in kindness and graciousness, then, heavy indeed is my heart.

How did doing the right thing become doing things because the boss will notice? Whatever happened to following one's heart? Is this what meritocracy really means? Why have Singaporeans not learned that, good or bad, we reap what we sow?

KEEPING HOPE ALIVE

These, then, are some of the lenses with which I look at my world and I use these lenses every day. There is a lot of joy in doing youth work but that work also comes with a heavy responsibility to always be on my best behaviour. I never know when a young person that I work with or that I may work with in the future might be watching! *Monkey sees and monkey does*, so I do try not to be the naughty, ungracious monkey. My reminder to myself is this admonishment from the Lebanese poet Kahlil Gibran: Whoever would be a teacher of men let him begin by teaching himself before teaching others; and let him teach by example before teaching by word.

The youth work I have done through many different public and private sector agencies in Singapore over the last dozen years has shown me that there are indeed many positive exemplars of gracious Singaporean youths. These lovely young people cut across gender, ethnicity and economic and educational backgrounds as well as other such social stratification indicators. Sadly, though, these positive exemplars are too few and far between, and getting lost in what I see as a swelling tide of ungraciousness among Singapore's young and not-so-young.

In my work with young people, I share with them two things I do that keep me optimistic and I ask them to see how they can make these part of their own lives. More important, I ask them to share these two things through their own words and deeds. These two things are what have kept me hopeful that Singapore can be a nicer place.

- *See the Good*

Realise that for every instance of negative behaviour that catches your attention, there are many more instances of expected or positive behaviours that have escaped your eyes. Our natural tendency is to notice negative exemplars so it takes conscious effort and practice to start to see the good without discounting it as atypical. We should always be mindful of the effects of unrepresentative exemplars on our constructions of social reality.

By no means am I deluding myself into believing that I live in a lovely place. But, seriously, there is no Utopia and Singapore really is not all that bad. Yes, there is plenty of social behaviour that makes me cringe but there are also lots of things I have seen and heard that give me cause to cheer. The question is how to make the cheer-worthy moments more commonplace.

- *Know Yourself, Govern Yourself*

If you remember nothing else about this presentation, I hope you will remember this: Know yourself, Govern yourself. Did you know that we are creatures of habit? Think about how you dress yourself each morning; which leg goes into the pants first? Which sock, which shoe? Graciousness begins with awareness. Not just awareness of the people around us, but of ourselves. We have to know ourselves and to acknowledge our own blots and spots. We have to know not just how we use language, but, also, how that language affects other people. We have to know how we speak with our hands, our eyes, our bodies and how these communicate what our words do not.

Young people who have come through my programmes will tell you I am a nag because I keep asking them to think through why they did or said something. We also need to govern or check ourselves. How do you respond when another driver tries to cut into your lane? Or when someone steps on your foot or bumps into you in a crowd?

In the face of ungracious behaviour, it is always our choice and entirely within our control whether we respond with grace and courtesy or with the same ungraciousness. We can plead all we want that "He started it!" But, seriously, the only behaviour, thoughts, and speech that you can control are your own. As Kahlil Gibran so eloquently put it: An eye for an eye and the whole world would be blind.

This has been a very personal narrative. I have offered you my attempts to make sense of ungracious behaviour, and the lessons I share with the young people with whom I work. I have also shared with you the reasons why I believe we can and should hold fast to the hope and belief that we can learn to be a more gracious people.

I will close this narrative by leaving you the following points to ponder:

- How can we be more *kiasu* about kindness and courtesy? Is it possible for us to be afraid to lose out when it comes to being gracious?

- How many more years will it be necessary for us to need kindness and courtesy campaigns to get Singaporeans to celebrate positive role models for more monkey-see, monkey-do in promoting graciousness?
- Can we chase after a more noble set of 5Cs, being Courtesy, Compassion, Consideration, Caring, and Courage to do the right thing for the right reasons?

I challenge you to embark on your own personal graciousness campaign. Just decide each week, what act or acts of kindness and courtesy you want to make extra effort to perform. Then, do it. And, get other people to join you as well!

Little would delight me more than to live in a Singapore society of *kiasu* monkeys who would cheerfully bring me chicken pies to welcome me home after a roadtrip. I would certainly do the same for them!

IV

One Global City

A global city is highly connected to the world and wields socio-economic influence through its many linkages. Several international indices have ranked Singapore amongst the world's top cities. This panel looks at what is required to sustain Singapore's success and maintain its economic competitiveness in a constantly changing global environment, especially given the increasing concerns over climate change and its implications for society. What are the economics of a global city in a region where every country wants to be a powerhouse? How does social stability in Singapore contribute to and reinforce the country's growing status as an important node in the global economy? Going into the future, is there a bright horizon for Singapore's growth strategies?

CHAPTER 9

One Global City

ANNIE KOH

The economics panel is the last panel for the day and is placed last because it is a critical panel. I have a wonderful group of speakers and, in a little while, I will tell you why you are so privileged.

As I sat through the discussions today, I realised that you have been a great audience. There is plenty of engagement but that is not good enough for me. As with all panels that I moderate, I require a higher level of engagement from those of you remaining in the hall at this juncture of the conference. The Global City is a very important theme and we will get increasingly global as Singapore moves forward. There is no running away from this phenomenon. From 2005 to 2009, 150,000 foreigners migrated to Singapore each year. We now have a population of five million and, by some estimates, a third of our 6.8% growth in the last five years came from the fact that we have a growing population.

This morning's first panel on "One United People" is essential because we will continue to see an influx of talented foreigners entering our shores and these individuals need to be engaged. That alignment in vision will enable Singapore to have a sustainable growth rate in the next ten years. I was delighted with the second panel discussion on "One Gracious Society". This panel discussion is relevant as it focuses on what it means to live in a city. I lived for four and a half years in New York City. I loved New York for its input and vitality but New York City also comes across then and now as very cold and impersonal. Therefore, as Singapore becomes increasingly globalised, how do we consciously strive to be a gracious society? How do we have it all — a lifestyle where everyone appreciates the excitement of city living and still practises the values of a kind and gracious society? Hence, this third panel today is most appropriate as it forms the core of the conversations we have been having today. Being global is inevitable for Singapore's survival.

We are going to commence with a wonderful friend, Mr Lee Kwok Cheong, who will share his perspectives as a leader of industry, seeing as he is Chief Executive Officer of SIM Global Private Limited and he had been a CEO of National Computer Systems (NCS) for ten years. This perspective is necessary as most companies every year measure an engagement index from the angle of a CEO asking certain critical questions about human capital in his company. The questions asked involve recruiting, developing and also retaining human capital. Singapore has only one resource — our human capital, home grown and from foreign shores.

Therefore, Mr Lee will be sharing his perspective on what kind of talent we are recruiting. How are we engaging and developing them and how we can continue to retain them so that they speak in one voice? Our next speaker, Mr Nizam Idris, is the first economist to speak in our conference today. He is the executive director and head of research and economic strategy at investment bank UBS. Mr Nizam is going to question if the Global City model is the only economically viable model for Singapore and, if so, what are some of the costs of being a Global City? How do we make Singapore a city to work, live, play and finally retire in, considering that it does not have a hinterland like London and New York City?

Ambassador Ong Keng Yong told us that every panel must have an academic point of view. We are therefore very privileged to have Professor Henry Yeung as the third speaker on this panel. He will be sharing with us his perspectives of Singapore as a Global City not in isolation, but one that needs to become increasingly engaged with its neighbours and involved in the network of different countries. What does this imply for Singapore as a Global City growing in terms of knowledge transfer and influence?

I look forward to the sharing and conversations from our esteemed panel.

CHAPTER 10

Beyond Economics for Economic Success

LEE KWOK CHEONG

INTRODUCTION

In his keynote address this morning, Prime Minister Lee Hsien Loong talked about three national challenges — economic restructuring, population and political renewal. Economic restructuring was seen as a nuts-and-bolts issue, while population was seen as a problem to be tackled. The points I wanted to make in the presentation I prepared — before I heard PM Lee's speech — were that our economic competitiveness could go beyond nuts-and-bolts factors, and that our changing demographics gives Singapore a unique solution rather than poses a problem. I do not disagree with PM Lee's perspectives, but I hope to offer an organising principle for consideration.

This is supposed to be an economic panel but I am not an economist. I am in the fields of Information Technology, education and business. I am sure the other learned panel members will bring relevant research data and insights. I will just be thick-skinned and offer my personal opinion.

Modern Singapore is an artificial construct. It has borrowed people, institutions, systems and ideas from many parts of the world. Hence it was a global village before the term was coined. The early success of Singapore has been mainly due to Singapore's good physical location and its strong government. As Finance Minister Tharman Shanmugaratnam said in a recent interview with *BusinessWeek* magazine, we "were not meant to come together as a country". A hundred years ago, fifty years ago, people came to earn a living here. They sent money home and planned to eventually return with sufficient savings. "Home" was somewhere else. It could have been a village in Malaya, Java, China, India or England.

We are still a young country, maybe a somewhat artificial one with a mixed group of people calling it home. Our challenge is how to sustain success in a constantly changing global environment. The previous sources of our people — China, India, Malaysia, Indonesia — now aspire to be successful global hubs in their own right. Why should people stay connected to Singapore? Let me state the obvious — our good location is no longer good enough. When 'bits' are more important than 'atoms', geographic location matters far less.

ATTRACTING AND RETAINING TALENT

In my work, I am always looking for thought leaders to share their views about Singapore. Where do I find these thought leaders? Mostly in two places. Firstly, in places of great natural beauty, with great weather and great outdoor activities, maybe somewhere remote, but connected to the world through information and communication technologies. This does not sound like Singapore, does it? The second place is in communities of interesting people and thriving ideas: this is something that Singapore can aspire to be.

Let me talk about some familiar iconic places. If you want to start up a technology venture, you go to Silicon Valley. If you want to be a movie star, you go to Hollywood. Each of these iconic destinations has its list of iconic heroes — the Steve Jobs and Tom Cruises. There is no coincidence that these places are in the United States, the land of the American Dream. These are places where you can become a star when you believe you can become someone extraordinary. These places allow you to pursue your dreams.

Let me make explicit what I have been assuming, based on the point above. Our future competitiveness depends largely on attracting talented people and keeping them connected to Singapore. I am not just talking about foreign talent but also talented Singaporeans who have a choice of going anywhere in the world. How do we attract them and keep them connected to Singapore? Let me borrow the metaphor "war for talent" in the context of organisations. Underlying all the fancy talk, this war boils down to three factors:

- **The job.** What do you do? What do you learn? How much do you earn?
- **The people.** The people you work with whom you spend more time than your family.
- **The culture.** Culture is what makes you feel you belong, what makes you feel proud to be part of a company and bonded to your colleagues. Culture takes a long time to establish in an organisation and is harder for competitors to copy than strategies, processes and systems.

If you get the three factors right, you capture the heart as well as the heads of people. We can apply the same metaphor to a country.

PLACE MARKETING SINGAPORE

Our panel topic is so big that it would take something like the high-powered Economic Strategies Committee and its sub-committees, working groups and secretariats to cover with a hundred recommendations. I can only offer two suggestions and to provide some sort of organising principle.

First, I would suggest that we give our old success formula of "location and people" a new definition. Namely, we can transform Singapore into an iconic destination, not by thinking of our location in geographical terms, but as a place that is "central in the mind", an iconic destination with people coming and staying for reasons pertaining to aspirations. Singapore's future prosperity depends on our continual efforts at re-inventing Singapore to add value to the global community. We have been a hub for goods, services and capital. Our future success will require us to be a hub for ideas and the imagination as well. This will happen only if we can harness the creativity of our people and project it globally.

How do we make Singapore an aspirational centre in the brand new world? I would like to offer my second perspective. The answer is in the people we have. I am not talking about what we do but who we are. What kinds of people do we have today? What different kinds of people are growing up in Singapore? I believe that demographics is destiny, although I also understand that not everyone subscribes to this dictum. The current demographic composition suggests that Singapore can become a hub for ideas and imagination if we *celebrate our diversity* rather than get fixated on racial and cultural fault lines.

CULTURAL DIVERSITY IN SINGAPORE

I would like to share my personal experience. I was born in Hong Kong. My wife was born in Japan. We met in Boston when we were students. We came to Singapore in 1983 as working professionals. We did not come as Chief Executive Officers. I stayed in a flat rented from the Housing Development Board. I paid $299 per month, which covered the conservancy charges. We found this place a little slow and boring back in 1983 but we felt very comfortable. Why did my wife and I come to Singapore? We do not know why. In retrospect, we felt unwelcomed in Hong Kong as a Chinese–Japanese couple speaking English to each other. Our eldest son is now working in New York. Our daughter did her degree in Australia and is now working in KK Women's and Children's Hospital. Our youngest son is a student in Nanyang Technological University. I am saying all these not because I want to talk about myself. I want to highlight that my example, though *very common in Singapore*, might be the exception in a homogenous society like Japan. These days you can throw a stone anywhere in Singapore and you find similar families to mine with such a *rojak* history.

These days we are familiar with the locals-versus-foreigners issue in Singapore. There are too many foreigners taking away jobs and places in schools. Some locals feel insecure and threatened. This is a political issue as well as an election issue. I am a little concerned that we are now talking like we are anti-immigrant. I will argue that when we look back 10 or 20 years from now, all these issues would be moot. We would have a large mix of the foreign-born and local-born in our population comprising different ethnicities in families, at homes, schools and workplaces. The distinctions would not matter.

An unscientific research I undertake daily now is to scan the obituaries in the newspapers. I have noticed an increasing mix of ethnicities in the list of family members of the deceased. The policy change earlier this month in the CMIO (Chinese, Malay, Indian and Others) model to allow mixed-race couples to register two races for their children might seem minor but it is inevitable. It is a fundamental change in who we are and what we are becoming.

Let us look at some data. An amazing statistic to me is that about half of the marriages registered in Singapore now are between citizens and non-citizens (see Figure 1). There is also an increasing trend of inter-racial marriages over the years. In 2009, such marriages formed 16% of all marriages.

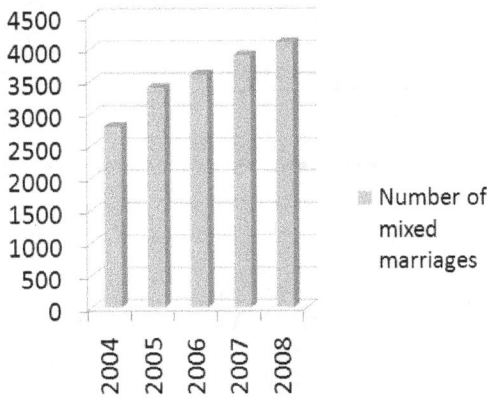

Figure 1 Changing face of marriage
Note: There has been a steadily-increasing trend of mixed marriages in Singapore.
Source: 'A Mix Up' [Infographic], *The Straits Times*, 4 Jan 2010

LOW FERTILITY RATE AND THE NEED FOR IMMIGRANTS

The government has decided to slow down the pace of bringing in foreigners. However, if we look at our Total Fertility Rate which is 1.28 (*Population in Brief: 2009*), which is way below the replacement rate of 2.1, the inconvenient truth we have to confront is we cannot sustain ourselves as a society without keeping our doors wide open to immigrants.

Coupled with the need for more immigrants, the next generation will see a sufficiently large proportion of the people in Singapore being multiracial, not only in exposure and outlook but also in their genes. To prevent the population from shrinking, this mixing will not stop anytime soon. Everything in our young country will become multi-hyphenated in the future and hopefully this will create a unique cultural experience which is *accepting and inclusive* without forcing assimilation into a dominant old culture.

Table 1

Year	Citizen Residents ('000)	PRs ('000)	Non-Residents ('000)
1990	2,624	112 1 per 23 citizens	311 1 per 8 citizens
2000	2,986	288 1 per 10 citizens	755 1 per 4 citizens
2009	3,201	553 1 per 6 citizens	1,254 1 per 2.6 citizens

Rapidly changing mix of citizens, permanent residents and non-residents
Source: *Population Trends 2009* from the Singapore Department of Statistics

SINGAPORE AS A GLOBAL CITY

I would like to show three tables used in the Economic Strategies Committee's Workgroup discussions which are also publicly available. Table 2 shows the ranking of cities according to the Global Cities Index, published in 2008. We rank highly in the economic dimension but not so highly in the cultural experience dimension.

Table 3 shows that we are behind leading cities in terms of museum attendance and the range of programmes and activities in our museums. How can Singapore become a vibrant and authentic home at the heart of Asia? Singapore can aspire to be a distinctive place that offers authentic culture, a vibrant landscape and diverse experiences, as well as being a liveable city offering its denizens the components which may lead to fulfilled lives. This way, Singapore may then build up a compelling international image.

I believe Singapore will be amongst a few global cities competing for business, investment, talent and influence. However, Singapore cannot be successful economically solely by having good infrastructure, tax incentives, education and training because other global cities also employ similar

Table 2

Ranking	City	Business Activity	Human Capital	Information Exchange	Cultural Experience	Political Engagement
				Dimension		
1	New York	1	1	4	3	2
2	London	4	2	3	1	5
3	Paris	3	11	1	2	4
4	Tokyo	2	5	7	7	6
5	Hong Kong	5	5	6	26	40
6	Los Angeles	15	4	11	5	17
7	Singapore	6	7	15	37	16
8	Chicago	12	3	24	20	20
9	Seoul	1	35	5	10	19
10	Toronto	26	10	18	4	24

Good in the economic but not the cultural experience dimensions
Source: The Global Cities Index, *Foreign Policy*, November/December 2008.

Table 3

	Singapore	New York	London
Admissions to major theatres in million / per capita	1.5 million / 0.3	12.3 million / 1.5	12.4 million / 1.6
Visitorship to top 5 museums / per capita	2.6 million / 0.4 per capita	8.3 million / 1.0 per capita	20.4 million / 2.4 per capita
Number of National Museums	3	16	22
Contribution to Economy	SGD164 million 4,500 jobs (For live performing arts and heritage only, 2006)	USD5.1 billion 44,000 local jobs (Broadway alone, 2006)	GBP1.1 billion 10,640 jobs (For City arts cluster, 2005)

Cultural sector in Singapore lags behind New York and London
Source: Economic Strategies Committee Subcommittee 5 Secretariat, 2009

economic strategies. I believe that a people rich in culture is also needed for Singapore to have an edge. If we can go beyond the traditional definition of talent and success, we will have a unique opportunity to create for ourselves a hard-to-copy competitive advantage. We will have good jobs. We will have interesting people. We just have to further develop our cultural experience.

SINGAPORE ICONS

What I suggest is for Singapore to establish icons to capture the imagination of the world. Icons invoke certain mental images of a place. They are a form of place marketing that presents our X-Factor to the world. What are examples of aspirational icon or icons that Singapore should have? When I asked myself this question, a few possibilities popped up, like The Great Wall, the Taj Mahal and the pyramids of Egypt and Petra. These icons are all symbols of the past. Some of you might suggest the Integrated Resorts and the Formula One night race as icons. Well, like the tallest buildings of the world, they will always be surpassed very quickly.

The giant panda is a good icon for China. Giant pandas are unique to China, given to other countries for goodwill. Maybe Singapore could do the same with our Merlion, if we could find live ones!

More important, however, are iconic heroes. Who do we believe are our heroes? Who do we put out there to the world as iconic heroes who represent the aspirations of Singapore? Who do we put out there to the world? Which iconic heroes represent the aspirations of Singapore? I would count Minister Mentor Lee Kuan Yew as one, but I would say that we have to move beyond him. I suggest we find others as well in other fields, like arts, sports and business, like the equivalent of Michael Jackson, Bill Gates and Tiger Woods. Singapore can also be an iconic city of interesting people — a cultural hybrid with varied cultural connections and a unique model of making a living and living a life.

CONCLUSION

We need to make Singapore a place that will capture the imagination of people so that they will want to stay because their hearts are here. I am not saying that we should disregard economic strategies. We will continue to work on them but we need to consider, for example, inspirational elements that make this place appeal to the heart and not just the head. In short, we need to go beyond hard economic strategies by looking at non-economic levers such as cultural influence, idea origination and soft power.

REFERENCES

The 2008 Global Cities Index, *Foreign Policy*, Nov/Dec 2008.

Population in Brief: Singapore Department of Statistics, Singapore, 2009.

Population Trends 2009, Singapore, 2009.

CHAPTER 11

The Future of Singapore as a Global City and its Socio-economic Implications

NIZAM IDRIS

Singapore is increasingly facing the direct opposite of the "oil curse" or the Dutch Disease that afflicts resource-rich countries. The "oil curse" basically led to the over-dependence on natural resources for growth and the neglect of human and other productive resources in the country with rich natural endowment. Singapore on the other hand is facing an over-dependence on human resource for growth. We import almost everything that we consume, from apples to zippers. Of these, foreign talent is perhaps the greatest and most important of our imports. But these cannot be imported at will or merely priced in dollars and cents; there has to be mutual consent. The people with the kind of talent we need must want to come to Singapore for the "transaction" to take place. For this, our economic policies have been geared towards making Singapore a great city to do business and to earn a living. But historically, a great city is not a great home and does not come with a great heart.

There is a price that comes with being great cities. Henry James, a British-American author, wrote of London in 1881 when he contemplated what was then, and still is, one of the greatest cities of the world, "It is not a pleasant place; it is not agreeable, or cheerful, or easy, or exempt from reproach. It is only magnificent." What makes a great city of the world is one of the paradoxes of history. Urban historian Lewis Mumford adds, almost reluctantly, that "when the worst has been said about urban Rome, one further word must be added: to the end, men loved her." The Bible described Babylon — generally acknowledged as one of the greatest cities of early human civilisations — as "the mother of harlots and abominations of the earth."

Singapore needs to be a great global city to be economically viable and sustainable. The alternative is being a mediocre, also-ran city that would never be able to attract the talent pool that would be needed to survive and compete without being a hub for manufacturing or natural resources. Economic policies are generally paving the way to make Singapore globally relevant. But recognising the potential pitfalls as we strive towards being a great city is equally important. How do we mitigate the impact of this growth model on our social fabric in the years ahead?

SUCCESSFUL GROWTH MODEL, WITH LOOMING PITFALL

Singapore's economic success has been nothing less than a marvel. Relentless capital accumulation, astute leadership and geographical advantage were the pillars to the country's success. But central to this success is the way the country has invested, nurtured and then more recently imported human resources to weave together these pillars into a cogent economic phenomenon. While I have little doubt that this economic growth-model, if maintained with a sound leadership, is destined for continued success, the implications on the broad social fabric of the nation could be put to test as the nation greys. One invariable side effect of a successful global city is the high cost of living. Without a hinterland to retreat to, ordinary Singaporeans may increasingly be deprived of comfortable retirements or worse, reasonable medical care in their autumn years. While we strive to enhance the economic success of the nation, we should not lose sight of this potential pitfall ahead.

Singapore's lack of natural resources left her with little choice but to invest heavily in its human resources and to attract and retain talent to fuel the economic drive. Fiscal spending on education has always been among the top item on the annual government budget. This is complemented by the drive to attract as many multinational corporations as possible from the manufacturing and banking industry to invest in and operate out of

Figure 1 Annual foreign direct investment flows into Singapore (US$ bn and as percentage of GDP)

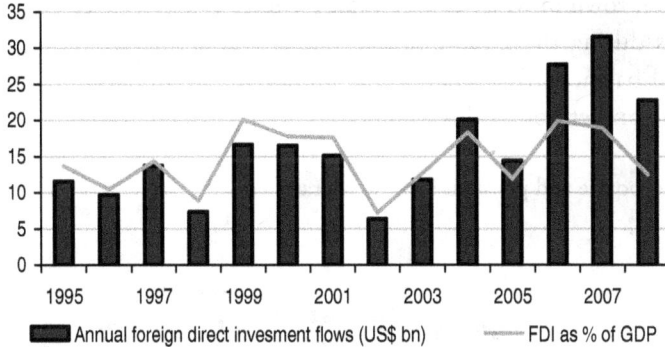

Trying to attract foreign investment puts Singapore in competition with other cities
Source: The Economic Survey of Singapore, Ministry of Trade and Industry, Bloomberg

Singapore as regional headquarters. To a certain extent this puts Singapore (Figure 1) in direct competition with other regional cities, particularly Hong Kong, for foreign direct investments and talents.

LOW TAX RATE

Attracting foreign capital and talent is key in boosting the growth potential of a small open economy with no natural resources, especially for a country like Singapore, which is also facing a dwindling citizen-fertility rate. An economy's potential output is always expressed as a function of the rate of change in population (labour force), capital accumulation and total factor productivity. Of these three factors Singapore has a clear advantage in attracting foreign talent given the country's open immigration laws. There is also no shortage in the talent that would consider Singapore as a base to further their career and to accumulate wealth in their productive years.

The usual methods used by global governments to attract foreign investors and talents are to make the country a liveable place with sound infrastructure and clean judiciary and executive arms. Broadly speaking, making Singapore a "great global city" is a key focus at attracting talent and investments.

One other potent tool to attract investments and foreign talents is to keep corporate and personal income tax rates low, with the occasional tax concessions thrown in when competition for foreign direct investment heats up, such as during the 2000/2001 economic recession. Given Singapore's strong fiscal balances, this was a viable option. Hong Kong again provides the sternest competition in this regard.

Figure 2 Corporate and personal income tax rates (%)

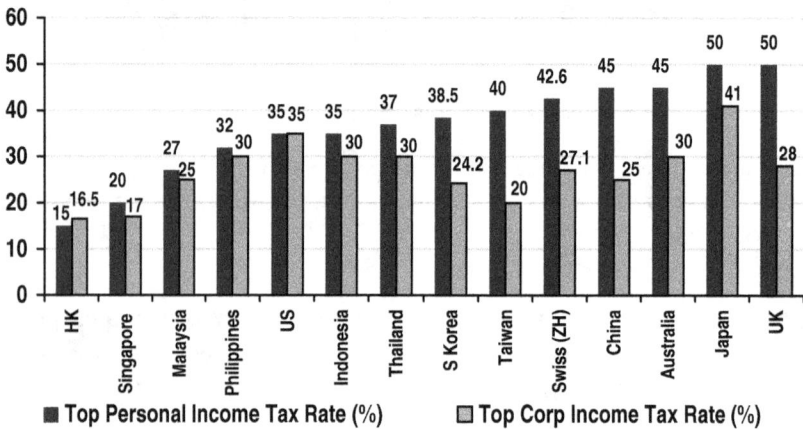

Singapore needs to keep corporate and personal income tax rates low to compete with the likes of Hong Kong

Sources: Australia Taxation Office, HK Inland Revenue Department, Japan National Tax Agency, Singapore Inland Revenue Authority, UK Inland Revenue, US Inland Revenue Service, www.forbes.com

AGEING POPULATION POSES FRESH CHALLENGES

On both counts Singapore has been successful. As a percentage of GDP, Singapore attracts one of the highest proportions of foreign investment globally. In 2008, foreign talent and labour accounted for 36% of the city-state's resident headcount. Indeed, data suggests Singapore has become increasingly dependent on foreign talent to maintain a high potential growth rate in recent years as the citizen population stagnates. In the last five years, for every one citizen born, we have seen more than nine inward immigrants adding to the population.

Figure 3   Contribution to average annual population growth (%)

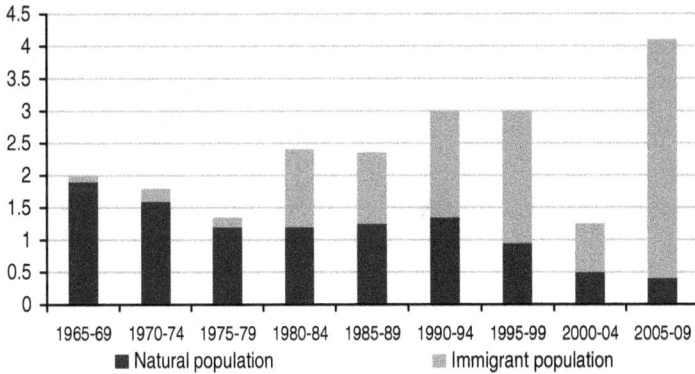

In the last three decades, Singapore's population has been bolstered by significant immigrant inflow
Source: Department of statistics; Ministry of Trade and Industry, United Nations

This is clearly a testimony to the successful efforts at making Singapore a great city to live in and to grow. Foreign workers are integral in Singapore's success. Presently, more than one in every three of the 4.84 million people who live, work and play in Singapore are non-citizens.

Figure 4   Singapore's population trend

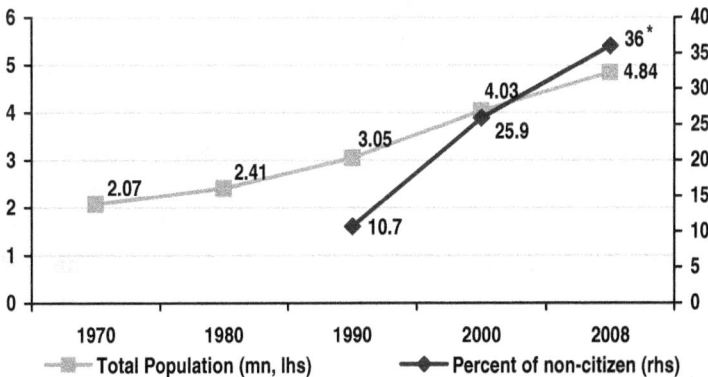

In 2008, 36% of Singapore's population was comprised of non-citizens
Source: Population trends, 2009; Department of statistics; Ministry of Trade and Industry; * estimate

Meanwhile the population is also ageing. Over the forty years to 2008, Singapore's population median age has almost doubled to 36.7 years. During the same time, the old-age support ratio — calculated as the number of population in the working age of 15–64 for every member of the population over the age of 65 — has almost halved to 8.4.

Figure 5 Demographic trend: Median age

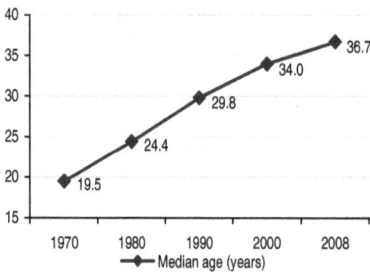

Figure 6 Old-age support ratio

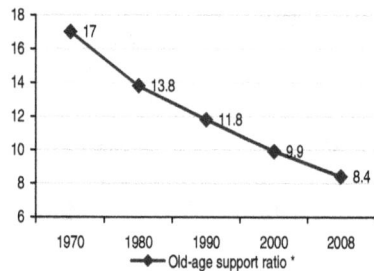

Source: Population trends, 2009, Department of Statistics; Ministry of Trade and Industry

Source: Population trends, 2009, Department of Statistics; Ministry of Trade and Industry;
* Number of population between 15–64 years old per elderly (> 65 years old)

As Singapore's population ages, the old-age support ratio has decreased in tandem

This statistic will fall further in the years ahead with the number likely to halve at a faster rate as the baby boomers reach retirement age. By my calculations based on the population trend numbers of the Department of Statistics, taking the Total Fertility Rate at 1.1 and keeping mortality and net migration equal to the average of the last 10 years[1], Singapore's old-age dependency ratio is set to fall to 4.0 in 30 years' time. Expressed differently, 20% of Singapore citizens will be at least 65 years old in 2040. This is only slightly lower than what Japan is currently experiencing.

---

[1] The methodology is consistent with that used by the Eurostat (http://epp.eurostat.ec.europa.eu) in making its long-term population projections. The methodological notes are detailed in a Mar 2006 paper: http://epp.eurostat.ec.europa.eu/cache/ITY_OFFPUB/KS-NK-06-003/EN/KS-NK-06-003-EN.PDF

Additionally, Singapore's low tax rate reduces the country's ability to provide an extensive social security network. The situation is exacerbated by the country's high expenditure on defence. Unlike Hong Kong which does not spend a single cent of its fiscal budget on defence, Singapore has spent approximately 26% of total fiscal expenditure (before transfers) or around 5% of GDP on defence over the last decade. The US spends an average of 3.8% of GDP or 17% of total federal budget on defence.

Unlike Japan which has a very closed immigration policy, Singapore is still likely to do well economically in 2040, thanks to Singapore's open immigration policy which is akin to that of the US. I am not at all concerned about the long-term viability of Singapore's economy. Rather it is the socio-economic implication of this model that worries me.

Figure 7 Demographic trend: age distribution, 1970

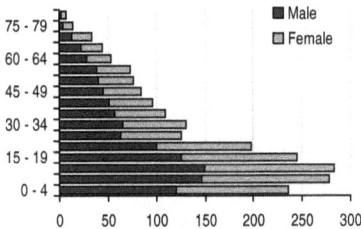

Source: Population trends, 2009, Department of Statistics; Ministry of Trade and Industry

Figure 8 Demographic trend: age distribution, 2008

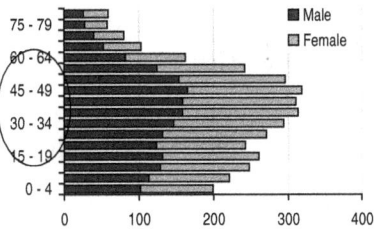

Source: Population trends, 2009, Department of Statistics; Ministry of Trade and Industry

UNAVOIDABLE HIGH COST OF LIVING

The other key statistic central to this thesis is the high cost of living inherent in a global city such as Singapore. Global cities attract the best talents to reside and work and the largest multinational corporations, which pay the highest wages to operate and establish regional headquarters. This is essentially what keeps Singapore ticking. Structurally, this also keeps Singapore's cost of living high.

According to the Mercer's Cost of Living Survey — a global survey which covers 143 cities across six continents and measures the comparative cost of over 200 items in each location, including housing, transport, food, clothing, household goods and entertainment — Singapore ranks as the tenth most expensive city in the world to live in. The Mercer's index suggests that the cost of living in Singapore is only marginally cheaper than that in New York City, and well ahead of regional neighbours such as Kuala Lumpur, Taipei, Seoul and even Sydney.

Table 1 Cost of living league

Position	Country	Index[*]	Position	Country	Index[*]
1	Tokyo	143.7	51	Seoul	79.9
4	Geneva	109.2	61	Taipei	78.2
5	Hong Kong	108.7	66	Sydney	75.5
8	New York City	100.0	96	Kuala Lumpur	69.2
9	Beijing	99.6	98	Bangkok	68.6
10	Singapore	98.0	105	Jakarta	64.9
			138	Auckland	54.0

Cost of living in Singapore is significantly higher than in other Asian metropolises
Source: Mercer's Cost of Living Survey, 2009

Singapore stands behind only other major global cities such as Tokyo, Geneva, Hong Kong, New York and Beijing in terms of living costs. But unlike these cities, Singaporeans do not have a hinterland to retreat to when their economic activity reduces with age or with illness. An American could work and accumulate wealth in New York but retire in Milwaukee, or if he does not like the cold, Florida, where the costs of living are significantly lower. In these states too one would get significantly higher level of state subsidies on healthcare and retiree supports. Likewise, an Englishman could work in London and retire in Yorkshire, a Japanese could work in Tokyo and retire in Sapporo. Such option is not available for Singaporeans, barring emigration. Emigration is however not always an option open to everyone, particularly the less well-off.

Not surprisingly the high cost of living also does not equate to high quality of life. Mercer's Global City Quality of Living Survey 2009, based on 39 factors including healthcare and other services, puts the quality of life in Singapore at 26, even though Singapore tops the infrastructure ranking in the same survey.

Table 2 Quality of living league

Position	Country
1	Vienna
2	Zurich
3	Geneva
4	Auckland
10	Sydney
2	**Singapore**

Singapore does not rank so high in quality of life despite its high cost
Source: Mercer's Quality of Living Global City Survey, 2009

This falling old-age support ratio and meagre social security network, made necessary by the low tax rates the country has had to maintain, would have profound socio-economic implications, particularly for a small city-state with no hinterland that offers a significantly lower cost of living for retirees to retreat to. This problem is arguably unique to Singapore given the need to keep tax rates low along with a high level of defence spending, thus making significant government subsidies for healthcare, retirement support and other social-security network disbursements not an option.

With limited government subsidies and social security network, many Singaporeans particularly the elderly, are one major illness away from bankruptcy. If my earlier calculations are even half right, this would be the case for a large proportion of our citizen population in 20 to 30 years' time. For a majority of Singaporeans, the pace of the rise in the cost of living has surpassed the rate at which their wages can possibly grow. Even subsidised housing costs have risen faster than the average growth in Singaporeans' income in annualised terms in recent years. This is likely to persist as more foreign talents reside in Singapore. With no real alternative to the current successful economic growth model, it seems pertinent that the Singapore government contemplates ways to mitigate the social impact of the economic model particularly on the elderly and the poor.

PROPOSAL: ONE BORDERLESS ASEAN

I realise that if one were to look at this issue from the political angle, this is probably not a major concern, especially if Singapore's economy will continue to be a phenomenal success for many years to come, as I suspect it will. We are often reminded by Singapore's leaders that a rising tide lifts all boats — a buoyant economy will trickle through to all layers of society. This is certainly true but this does not mask the fact that life at the bottom half of the earning spectrum will be increasingly hard even as income continues to rise.

Politics and charity are seldom spoken in the same breath; the former is often an arena for the elites. I am not naïve to think that politics should not be separated from ethics. But it is only in focusing on the socio-economic impact of our growth policy that these factors become a deep concern.

With no cheaper alternative or hinterland to live in, it is already increasingly hard for Singaporeans to retire comfortably. More elderly citizens are seen working in fast food restaurants or as janitors and cleaners in offices and food centres around the island. We are fast approaching the end of retirement as we know it.

But working till one drops is not a viable option for many with low skill and education levels, which will apply to a high proportion of Singaporeans who will reach 65 years or older in 20 years' time. The social implication of this ageing group with ever smaller support network is likely to be profound.

One alternative is to work towards a borderless ASEAN (Association of Southeast Asian Nations). This would not only provide Singapore access to talent from the region and a market of total population size of 580 million, but perhaps more importantly with a vast "hinterland" for retiring Singaporeans to migrate to and live comfortably and more fully in their autumn years.

But forging a borderless ASEAN still seems daunting given the varied stages of development of the member countries, with numerous examples of vested interests often hindering major multi-lateral decisions that the grouping has aimed for in recent years. We could start with a smaller union of Malaysia and Singapore, but with each country retaining clear autonomy over domestic policies; a "one federation, two systems" of sorts. There would have to be no question of subordination as this is unlike the formation of Malaya between 1946 and 1963. This would be more akin to the European Union: while Brussels is the capital of the EU, France does not have to pay homage to Belgium.

This arrangement could then be gradually expanded to include more of the ASEAN member nations. This would foster greater cooperation and understanding among member countries and ownership of the region, which would likely reduce the defence spending for member countries such as Singapore. Such savings could be used to enhance the availability of social security support networks in each country.

During the seminar I was asked where I would retire. My short answer was Singapore. That I believe is what most of us would like. But the reality is probably harsher with the cost of living likely to be beyond our current imagination by 2030. I may even rule out retirement altogether with most of my savings spent on medical care and little left for inheritance. If, on the other hand, the idea of a borderless ASEAN comes into fruition in the next 20 to 25 years, retiring in the lower-cost regional countries would be a very alluring option, giving me the opportunity to live a fuller life with fewer financial worries. Cashing in on all my assets and savings (with tax fully paid), I would love the idea of retiring comfortably in Cambodia with enough money to start and run a school or a hospital to help the less fortunate among our neighbouring countries. Others may consider a simpler retirement life in places such as East Java or a northern Malaysian state. These options offer more fulfilling and meaning conclusions to one's lives both spiritually and socially rather than having to work till the last breath. How one wishes to spend one's autumn years is a matter of personal choice. The important thing is that Singaporeans need to have that something better than the Hobson's choice of working till one drops or destitution.

CHAPTER 12

Globalising Singapore: One Global City, Global Production Networks and the Developmental State

HENRY WAI-CHUNG YEUNG

INTRODUCTION

The fact that city-states are globalising is not new. What is surprising, however, is that much of the existing understanding of global cities has paid only lip service to the complex inter-relationships between global city formation and the developmental state. This lacuna in our understanding, particularly through popular discourses and media reports, can be largely explained by the dependency of these stories on two to three exemplary global cities — London, New York and, occasionally, Tokyo. This skewed representation of global cities is indeed misleading, if not outright wrong, in today's inter-dependent global economy. I believe there is an urgent need to extend our existing understanding by incorporating other varieties of global city formation and by investigating, in historically and geographically specific ways, the processes through which these other global cities are formed, transformed, and extended beyond their immediate urban territoriality. The aim of this chapter, therefore, is to explore the inter-relationships between global city formation and the developmental state in the context of Singapore's global reach. "Global reach" is defined as the diverse processes through which a city articulates itself into and benefits from participation in the global economy.

By examining the rise of global cities in relation to their dynamic articulation into the global economy, I consider the global connections and outward orientation of dynamic cities rather than just their internal characteristics. My approach to "globalising cities" contrasts with the existing influential understanding of global city in both academic studies and public discourses, which focuses primarily on the internal attributes of talents and creative cities, particularly those associated with the influential arguments put forward by public intellectuals such as Saskia Sassen, Richard Florida and Charles Landry. I argue that we need to investigate how processes and mechanisms internal to global cities are coupled in strategic ways with the transnational network relations beyond these cities. In other words, we should be concerned with how a global city comes into being rather than merely accounting for its internal attributes. By unpacking this process of "coming into being", we can have a better sense of what the future might look like for the global city.

To illustrate my approach in the context of Singapore as a global city-state, I examine the case for developing Singapore as an innovative knowledge cluster in the global economy. I show how Singapore has been strongly embedded in evolving regional divisions of labour spearheaded by lead firms in global production networks. Singapore's articulation in these global production networks is contingent on its unique political-economic-urban configuration as a global city-state. By deploying its powers and capacities as a nation-state to transform society and space within the city, Singapore has successfully embedded itself within the evolving lattice of network relations that propel the global knowledge economy. Existing space and social formations are purged, restructured, and replaced by "world-class" infrastructure, education, legal, financial, and healthcare systems. The city-state of Singapore has therefore harnessed the benefits from creative cluster development that offers significant economic synergies and economies of scale and scope to enhance high-tech and knowledge-intensive development potential through a peculiar combination of institutional support, foreign investment, and local knowledge development. Unlike their counterparts elsewhere in industrialised economies, innovative clusters in Singapore represent a deliberate and state-driven attempt to attract the location of high-tech or knowledge-intensive activities by transnational corporations and local enterprises.

THE EMERGENCE OF SINGAPORE AS GLOBAL CITY-STATE

To a large extent, city-states such as Singapore and Hong Kong are unique historical and geographical realities because the state is contained within a fully urbanised and spatially constrained territorial unit. The national and the urban/local scales are effectively juxtaposed. Global city-states are clearly different from other global cities (for example, London and New York) because they do not have an immediate hinterland *within* the same national territorial boundaries. To a significant degree, broader regions (for example, Southeast Asia in the case of Singapore) and more distant parts of the globe become their hinterland. The development of a terrain of extraterritorial influence emerges when the global city-state functions like established global cities, both in attracting material and non-material flows, and in functioning as a command and control centre for the flows and networks that reach out at regional (for the most part) and, sometimes, global scales. Not surprisingly, global city-states play key roles as international financial centres, acting as the basing sites for the intermediaries of global finance. The strong financial role of the global city-state is a key contributing factor to the Alpha ("the brightest") status accorded to Singapore by the Globalization and World Cities (GaWC) Research Network ('The World According to GaWC", 2009 revised version) based in the United Kingdom's Loughborough University, the world's leading academic think-tank on cities in globalisation.

Unlike other municipal governments in leading global cities, Singapore has virtually direct access to the global economy. State policies can be shaped to develop the city-state into a global city-state. This process implies that Singapore must be not only an attractive location for material inflows from the global economy, but also be an *origin* of development flows (versus mainly repatriated profits) and innovative ideas to participate in the global economy. The term "global reach" best captures the dynamics of Singapore's global city-state formation pathway. It illustrates how a specific territorial organisation (for example, the city-state) is able to extend its influence and relations in the global economy through encouraging both inward and outward flows of people, ideas, capital, goods and services, and information.

Singapore differs from established global cities such as London and New York in at least three important ways. First, the global city-state has the political capacity and legitimacy to mobilise strategic resources to achieve national objectives that are otherwise unimaginable in non-city-state global cities. This is the case because as a city-state, Singapore is represented and governed by the state in all of its roles. When one recognises that a unified state in city-states plays all of these roles, including the creation and governance of financial markets and the management of territorial boundaries, and that the territoriality of governance is miniscule in comparison to most nations — it takes 45 minutes to drive a car from one side of Singapore to the other — the unique nature and capacities of the global city-state becomes all the more evident. This is an issue that development planners in larger nations — for example, Sydney in Australia and Tokyo in Japan — are well aware of since these global cities are governed in a relatively more complex, less coherent, and less strategic fashion. The leading cities in these larger nations are often confronted with complex inter-city politics that are absent in a city-state.

Second, and on a related note, the direct access to the global economy enjoyed by Singapore enables it to devise and implement strategic "UrbaNational" policies to gain sustainable national/urban competitiveness. The global city-state is not constrained by the tensions inherent in national-versus-urban politics or regional development politics confronting so many developing and, for that matter, developed countries that aspire to "construct" their global cities (for example, Shanghai versus Beijing). In other words there are no other regions or cities within the same country competing for material and non-material resources. The politics of city/nation-building tends to be focused on the strengths and weaknesses of policy options rather than which intra-national territorial unit is deserving of attention and resources.

Third, the most prominent of these global city-states — Singapore and Hong Kong — are the products of colonialism, and then postcolonial political dynamics. Colonial origins helped to shape urban destinies that were, and still are tightly intertwined with the evolving global economy. This colonial history has helped to bring about an openness to constant change and an outward-oriented and relatively cosmopolitan sensibility. Colonialism also helped to lay the legal, linguistic, and technological (especially transport) foundations for integration into the contemporary global economy. Finally, postcolonial political dynamics — especially the 1965 ejection of Singapore from Malaysia — concentrated the minds of politicians on the necessity of pursuing the global city pathway years before academics and planners were speaking of the global city or the world city.

How does Singapore acquire the capacity to spur itself in its global reach? While there are a variety of factors to consider in such a discussion, it is clear that we must turn our attention to the building of institutional capacities in the global city-state of Singapore. In particular, two inter-related aspects of this process of building institutional capacities stand out clearly: developmentalism and political control. Whereas a global city-state may serve the global economy well through its role as a command and control node, the nation state may have certain developmental objectives that run against the call for putting the global logic of capital above the local/national interests of its citizens and residents. To accomplish these contradictory objectives of caring for citizens and serving the global economy, the Singapore state often takes on a developmental role. Developmentalism and the developmental state may sometimes be a historical legacy in Asia (for example, in Japan and South Korea). They may also be a consequence of intense political struggles that end with the dominance of one political power or coalition. Their emergence is therefore highly specific within particular historical and geographical contexts.

At a national scale, a developmental state that satisfies these conditions has a much greater capacity to effect global reach in the building of an exploitable extraterritorial terrain in the aim of benefiting the city-state, while simultaneously enhancing the formation of global linkages via the attraction of foreign direct investments and foreign firms. In Singapore, a plethora of state-directed institutions, policies, programmes, and projects have emerged to spur the outward investment process. This is due in part to the historical underdevelopment of indigenous entrepreneurship in the private sector, which has convinced the state that regionalisation drives cannot be effectively taken up by private sector initiatives only.

Focusing inwards, the political power and control of the developmental city-state of Singapore distinguishes it from municipal governments in most global cities because it is able to bypass national-state/provincial-city politics typical in many global cities. In Singapore, for example, immigration policies and borders can be tightly managed to facilitate labour market restructuring — a capacity that no other global city has. On land use planning matters, the Urban Redevelopment Authority (URA), the statutory board responsible for urban planning, answers directly to the Ministry of National Development. In turn, one key agent of national development, the Economic Development Board (EDB), has near-monopoly power in determining the strategic direction of the economy. Given that the EDB formulates and implements national economic development policy, and the URA then falls in line to ensure land use planning supports EDB directives, the politics of urban change is highly charged, hierarchical in nature, and rarely becomes complicated by citizen involvement procedures. A further consequence of intertwining the national and the urban is that all urban planning policies, programmes, and projects are suffused with the politics of nation-building in the postcolonial era. More pragmatically, 100% of the country/city is planned by one authority, with every square centimetre of the city being managed in a fine-grained manner.

Singapore is thus simultaneously urban, national as well as global in its governance functions. The state is able to acquire discursive power by mobilising citizens and residents towards a common national goal, for example, becoming a global city. It can evoke the globalisation discourse to legitimise political, economic, and, in some cases, even social policies. Take the recent debate on immigration and population policies, for example. Referring to his encounter in Singapore in the early 1990s, John Friedmann, one of the best-known authorities on global cities, reflected that

> A few years ago, I was invited by the government of Singapore to speak on world cities. In private conversations with senior government officials it became clear to me what the government really wanted. Singapore was embarking on 'the next lap' (Government of Singapore, 1991), and officials hoped to hear from me how their city state might rise to the rank of a 'world city'. The golden phrase had become a badge of status, just as 'growth poles' had been in an earlier

incarnation. *There was little I could say that the government did not already know.*"[1]

The fact that a global city guru like Friedmann was consulted by Singapore's URA points to a legitimising practice of the latter in order to get the state's "next lap" of urban planning policy endorsed by this world-class expert. The state planning authority would then be able to put "expert" legitimacy in such planning documents as *Living the Next Lap* published by the Urban Redevelopment Authority in 1991.

Given the role of the state *vis-à-vis* the limited size of the territory being governed, Singapore's global city formation process has been both rapid and unique. State-guided urban restructuring, in the context of the rapid development of the Asia-Pacific over the last three decades, has facilitated the formation of deep and complex global economic linkages and interdependencies. The juxtaposition of both national and city governance in the hands of the developmental city-state of Singapore necessarily implies that it is also able to extend its control over most aspects of social and political life of its citizens. The net outcome of this control is that the state is able to mobilise social actors and tremendous resources to meet its national objectives (for example, global reach and creative city). It is also able to eliminate major opposition to its developmental policies through social control and discursive practices. Under these circumstances, the nation state becomes the city and the city becomes the nation state. The global reach of the city-state becomes an institutional extension of the influence and relations of the nation state on a global scale. It should be noted that not all actors in a city-state, and not all city-states, are willing and/or able to initiate and complete such processes of global city formation. Much depends upon existing political-economic and social-organisational processes, the capability of key actors (firms, state, and institutions) in exercising power to implement certain strategies that situate the city-state in a beneficial manner to the global spaces of flows, and the complex and intertwined influences of history and path dependency.

---

[1] The emphases in Friedmann's quote are mine.

BEYOND 2010: FROM GLOBAL CITY-STATE TO A GLOBAL INNOVATIVE KNOWLEDGE CLUSTER

How then do innovative clusters in Singapore emerge in the above context of global city formation? To locate sector-specific global production networks in these clusters, we need to bring in global lead firms and other relevant actors and show how selected industrial clusters grow hand-in-hand with the activity of these lead firms. This story shows the pathways taken by Singapore to achieve high-tech urban development. In particular, we need to pay special attention to the changing post-war economic development strategies in Singapore, thereby showcasing how state institutions matter in shaping the national system of technological innovation and in chartering a unique pathway to economic development.

Unlike their counterparts elsewhere in industrialised economies, creative clusters in Singapore represent a deliberate and state-driven attempt to attract the location of high-tech activities by transnational corporations and local enterprises. Aiming to create specific places to ground globalising research and development (R&D) activities, the Singapore government has encouraged cluster formation through various initiatives to generate agglomeration economies for R&D activities (e.g. superior physical infrastructures, generous financial incentives, and the proximity of universities and research institutes). These initiatives are predicated on a peculiar assumption about the spatiality of innovation and knowledge development inherent in the cluster model:

(i) R&D activities typically cluster in geographically favourable locations
(ii) there should be spatial contiguity or proximity among those elements of the innovation process located in the clusters.

One would imagine that such agglomeration economies and cluster advantages might be better enhanced and reaped through deliberate government policies at the urban scale (a global city advantage), as evident in Singapore's relative success in industrialising the nation and the city.

Singapore's transition towards a knowledge-based economy points to the complex interaction between global production networks and creative clusters at the urban level. Through the cross-border activities of lead firms and their strategic partners, industrial clusters in Singapore are plugged into dynamic global production networks. More specifically, the experience of Singapore's hard disk drive, petrochemicals, and biomedical industries shows that creative clusters do not emerge as pure agglomeration in a natural and taken-for-granted sense. Instead, they are deliberate creations in the context of supportive government policies (free trade regimes and significant investment in education), institutional structures (pro-foreign business environment), and cost conditions (lower labour and land costs). The key impetus to their formation and transformation comes from external actors such as lead firms and their strategic partners in global production networks.

To move beyond 2010, we need a revised model to foster the emergence of knowledge clusters within creative cities. Such a model must include both local and non-local links in each of these creative clusters. Those local links are related to such agglomeration economies as the existence of a local pool of cheap or specialised labour, the provision of non-traded inputs through talents, knowledge infrastructure, subsidies or grants, and access to local markets. However, these local links are insufficient in explaining the existing formation and future evolutionary growth of such creative clusters in global cities. We need also to understand their *competitive* position in global production networks which are mediated through non-local links, such as firm-specific organisation of value-chain activity. From such a global production network perspective, creative clusters in cities such as Singapore emerge to fulfil specific and yet complementary functions in particular global value chains. I have also previously used the concept "strategic coupling" to explain such co-production of knowledge clusters. Such functional links are external to individual clusters and often ignored in existing popular discourses on clusters and creative cities.

Singapore's experience in chartering its peculiar pathway to high-tech and knowledge-intensive industrialisation since the 1980s is unique among newly industrialised economies in Asia. Its *entrepôt* status and the state's pursuit of an export-oriented industrialisation strategy have inevitably articulated the city-state into the global economy. And yet the state in Singapore has been able to intervene in the market economy to develop a unique repertoire of innovative capacity in various sectors and clusters of the national urban economy. By carefully managing the development of knowledge clusters as a spatial congregation of research and development activities, supplier networks as collaborators in high-tech production orchestrated by foreign transnational corporations (TNCs), and industrial clusters as a core pillar of Singapore's manufacturing industries, the developmental city-state continues to harness global forces to its own advantage. To a certain extent, Singapore's national innovation and knowledge system can be regarded as a highly coordinated and managed system that brings together contributions from the developmental state, foreign TNCs, and local enterprises. Such a unique tripartite combination of actors distinguishes Singapore's case from other innovation systems and creative cities in advanced industrialised economies where local enterprises and state institutions remain the main actors in economic development.

IMPLICATIONS FOR FUTURE PUBLIC POLICIES

One clear lesson from this chapter is that the replicability of global city models is in serious doubt and the call for many countries to attain global city status is unfounded. Global cities should not be viewed as an end-state phenomenon or some kind of achievement, but should be seen as an evolving process resulting in highly divergent urban formation and transformation. Striving for global city status is like shooting a moving target. While such hyper-global cities such as London and New York continue to reinvent themselves to service their global network of cities and their governance, emerging global cities will find it very difficult to replicate the success of London and New York as centres of excellence in the command and control of the global economy. On the other hand, global city-states such as Singapore should continue to pursue "UrbaNational" developmental strategies by reaching the wider global economy via material and knowledge linkages. The success of these strategies is not predicated on an essential "global city strategy". There is no cookbook approach to global city formation. Rather, their success is determined by the institutional capabilities and political will of the city-state in effecting its global reach. I believe it is the construction of these capabilities and willpower, not their predetermined outcomes as a result of pursuing global city formation that will matter in the future of Singapore as a global innovative knowledge cluster. In other words, whilst global city formation may be deemed highly desirable by the development state of Singapore, whether we can sustain our relative position as a global city remains an event highly dependent on historically and geographically specific contexts.

This analysis of Singapore as a globalising city-state has important policy implications for its future development that extends well beyond its pivotal role in the global economy. I think continual and sustained strategic engagement with the global economy will pose significant challenges to the existing economic policies and practices in Singapore. The key issues to the future of Singapore's competitiveness as a global city-state are related to the kind of "UrbaNational" innovation system and the role of the state. First, Singapore's national innovation system needs to be much less coordinated and managed from the above. As the global economy's focus moves increasingly further away from Anglo-American economies in the post-2008 financial world, a great deal of uncertainties and possibilities will emerge in the future global landscape of demand for knowledge and innovation. The developmental state is perhaps not in the best position to capitalise on this fluid yet challenging scenario, due to its inherent institutional rigidities and path dependency. Instead, a myriad of non-state actors, such as business firms, R&D institutions, industry associations and so on, can play a much more effective role in fashioning a national innovation network in which the global city knowledge cluster in Singapore is well-embedded. This more decentralised approach is not easily acceptable to economic and urban planners in the Singapore state, as historical experience has locked them into a particular mindset that may indeed go against innovation and creativity. The challenge in the future lies in how to harness the creative power and innovative synergy of non-state actors in fostering a sustainable future for Singapore as a global city-state.

This call for less state coordination does not mean the end of the state in Singapore's economic future. Instead, what has emerged from my analysis in this chapter is that the developmental state in Singapore has always been putting political credibility and policy consistency as the top priorities in its engagement with global capital and in managing economic forces associated with globalisation tendencies. This institutional capacity can be sustained through its labour and financial market governance. In both markets, the state has consistently managed flexibility and domestic interests to attract global capital. Its ability is predicated on the character and legitimacy of domestic institutions, not on the alleged external pressures created by globalisation pressures. While the state and its myriad of associated institutions cannot possibly guarantee the future success of Singapore's transition to a global innovative knowledge cluster, its accumulated capacity to effect changes and transformations can be crucial to the continuous remaking of Singapore's political economy into something that might just be more resilient and versatile in the face of growing global competition, especially in the context of the post-2008 state stimulus packages. In this way, the powerful combination of both the global city — as represented by a diverse mix of local and non-local flows and actors — and the city-state can unleash a new growth dynamic that might sustain our economic future in the next decades to come.

REFERENCES

Friedmann, John (1995). Where we stand: a decade of world city research, *World Cities in a World System*, Paul L. Knox and Peter J. Taylor (eds.). Cambridge: Cambridge University Press.

Olds, Kris and Yeung, Henry Wai-chung (2004). Pathways to global city formation: a view from the developmental city-state of Singapore, *Review of International Political Economy*, Vol. 11, No. 3, pp. 489–521.

Yeung, Henry Wai-chung (2006). Understanding Singapore's global reach: outward investment trends, firm-specific motivations, and government policies, *East Asian Economic Perspectives*, Vol. 17, No. 2, pp. 40–77.

Yeung, Henry Wai-chung (2006). Innovating for Global Competition: Singapore's Pathway To High-Tech Development, in *Asian Innovation Systems in Transition*, Bengt-Åke Lundvall, Patarapong Intarakumnerd and Jan Vang (eds.). Edward Elgar, Cheltenham.

Yeung, Henry Wai-chung (2005). Institutional capacity and Singapore's developmental state: managing economic (in)security in the global economy, in *Globalisation and Economic Security in East Asia: Governance and Institutions*, Helen E S Nesadurai (ed.). London: Routledge.

Yeung, Henry Wai-chung (2010). *Globalizing Regional Development in East Asia: Production Networks, Clusters, and Entrepreneurship*, Regions and Cities Series No. 41, London: Routledge.

Globalization and World Cities Research Network (GaWC). The World According to GaWC, June 2009 (revised version). <http://www.lboro.ac.uk/gawc/world2008.html>, accessed on 26 January 2010.

SECTION **V**

Conclusion

13

Closing Address: Be Open to All Possibilities

ONG KENG YONG

There are many things to be said arising from this year's Singapore Perspectives conference, but let me try to do a five-minute wrap-up of the day. And I would like to invite Professor Tommy Koh to say a few words after this. He has been our guru and IPS has been indebted to him for all the work, time and effort he has given to the Institute. I told him he has only five minutes so that we all leave this room on schedule!

My takeaway from each of the sessions of this Singapore Perspectives 2010 is as follows. I thought the Prime Minister's speech this morning was very "directional", to borrow the word used by Lee Kwok Cheong in the panel earlier. His speech really shows that the leadership in Singapore has an open mind, especially in finding the solutions to the challenges facing us.

For the first panel on "One United People", I thought that there was not enough focus on the political questions. Actually, whether it is the melting-pot, mosaic or multicultural model for our multicultural society that is under discussion, each of them, and the kind of identities that they imply, is tied to some political consideration. And Singapore is a very politicised place. Although many people believe that we do not seem like a very politicised system given the longevity of and the way the ruling party has been able to determine narratives and policies in this country, my view is that it actually is very politicised. Hence I thought we should have had more discussion on what the political considerations are with regard to some of these possibilities that the panel speakers talked about.

I feel that pluralism will be what defines Singapore as we go forward, and every one of us should start to know what it means to be part of a pluralistic society and how we can accommodate all our respective views and concerns whether we are Chinese, Malay, Indian and Others, or whether we are Muslims, Hindus, Christians, Buddhists and so on.

I enjoyed the second panel on "One Gracious Society". I like the point made about whether we should be living graciously or just be contented with having gracious living. At the end of the day, these values will determine how Singapore and what Singaporeans will be like in the coming years. Campaigns in the past have been prescriptive, but we should have an open mind with regard to how we approach such campaigns. "Campaign" is not a dirty word; it has a lot of value. I believe that all of us must try to be educated, and that means we have to take responsibility and look at how we interact with people, how we relate to our country and our society in the manner befitting someone who has received a good education, or as some would say, "nine years of schooling". Very often I find that it is impossible to describe Singaporeans as "educated", especially when you see the way they litter our beaches and the areas around fast food outlets. I have tried on a few occasions to tell people who had left litter around Starbucks and McDonald's and each time my wife was ready to dial the police because she was afraid that I would be beaten up!

You just heard the last panel, "One Global City". What we have to bear in mind is that Singapore, whether we like it or not, is subjected to many influences. Technological progress is also an important issue here. That is why we have, in our policy circles, talked about "the Singapore Bypass": an aeroplane today can fly people from Australia all the way to Europe in one straight flight. Very soon, if we are not careful, no one will stop in Singapore, no one would need to be in Singapore. And that would be disastrous for us. This is one of the strategic concerns that we have in mind when we scenario-play and think about Singapore 30 years down the road. And according to what we know the technology that will bypass Singapore is already here, so we do not need 30 years. It could happen in the next ten years.

Hence it is important for us to adopt an open mind, to change our mindsets, to transform ourselves, and find ways to pull all these things together. I hope your takeaway from this conference is that overall, we

Singaporeans as host to many of the foreign talents and guest workers in Singapore have many good things in our favour, and it is just how we can pull all these things together and make the best out of it. I believe that if we can pull all these things together, consolidate ourselves, we will have a good and prosperous future. There is no need to feel insecure about all these new elements around us. It is part of our society being exposed to what is happening around us, and we have to make the best of all these influences and technological developments just as our parents and forefathers did in shaping this country from a relatively unknown port and fishing village.

Ladies and gentlemen, I hope you have enjoyed this conference as much as I did. We have brought to you several thought-provoking perspectives from all our speakers. For instance, what Nizam Idris suggested in the last panel about "one federation, two systems". It is meant to tease you. He is not saying that this is the only way forward. Nowadays you do not have to be contiguous to one another to form countries. It could also be that Singapore could team up with other like-minded countries or global cities around the world.

So, what I am trying to suggest to all of you is that be open, look at all possibilities, and try to see how you, your friends, your family, your circle and your community can play a role in making this place a much better place than what you have now. The young generation of Singapore has to carry on, and this is the reason why I have asked my colleagues, the young colleagues at IPS, to run this Conference this year.

Now, I must feature our guru, Professor Tommy Koh. Professor Koh has guided IPS for many years. Recently we merged with the Lee Kuan Yew School of Public Policy and re-organised ourselves, including making Professor Koh our Special Adviser. It is only right that we hear him sum up what he is taking away from this Conference.

14

Closing Remarks

TOMMY KOH

I was not planning to say anything today but since Keng Yong has very generously requested me to bring this successful Perspectives to a sweet conclusion, I will follow my wife's good advice and make three points.

First, I want to thank Keng Yong for empowering our young colleagues in the Institute of Policy Studies by entrusting to them the responsibility for conceptualising this year's Perspectives. I do not know whether you have noticed it or not, but Keng Yong has also empowered women, because the chairpersons of all three panels today — Pek Siok Lian, Paulin Tay Straughan and Annie Koh — are women.

Second, I was very encouraged this morning by one remark which Prime Minister Lee Hsien Loong made. When talking about the need to make all Singaporeans feel that this is their home and that they are all stakeholders, he said we should encourage Singaporeans to have greater empathy and to demonstrate support for our less fortunate citizens through philanthropy, volunteerism, corporate social responsibility and individual acts of kindness. I think this is a very important statement coming from the PM.

I think the need for social cohesion is important in our context, in which Singapore has no choice but to continue to import foreign talent, to make up for our deficit. I think it is impossible for a developed society to have a high birth rate. There is no country in the world, which is economically advanced and which has a high birth rate. So, in order to convince Singaporeans to not feel threatened by the large numbers of immigrants and new Singaporeans, I think we need to pass what I would call the "Taxi Driver's Test". My American friends, who visit Singapore, say to me that it is not true that people are afraid to talk about politics in

Singapore. Whenever they take a taxi from Changi Airport to their hotels, they say that the taxi drivers in Singapore are outspoken critics of the government. The taxi drivers are, in a sense, representatives of our heartlanders. They work long hours, about 12, and earn a modest income, less than $2,000 a month. Life is hard for them and their families. We have to devise social policies to ensure that the taxi drivers and their families, and others like them, are able to benefit from the rising tide. In this respect, we should worry about the growing disparity and the social stratification of our society. We have to raise the standard of living of the bottom 40% of our social pyramid.

My takeaway from Panel Two is that campaigns work best when they are driven by multiple stakeholders with the government playing the role of the lead stakeholder. In the past, campaigns were driven singly by the government. I think Terence Chong was probably right when he said that those days are over. We now live in a new world, a less hierarchical world, a world in which the government is still very important, but so are the people. I think that in future campaigns, the new wisdom is that all campaigns ought to be driven by multiple stakeholders.

Let me just conclude by sharing with you my takeaway from the final panel. I am very optimistic about Singapore's future, and I want to share with you the reasons for my optimism.

I feel that in the new world, national borders are becoming less and less important. We live in an increasingly borderless world. If you do not have enough territory, you can always use the territory of other countries, either by building industrial parks in those countries or through joint ventures or foreign direct investment. If you do not have enough people, you do not have to import large numbers of foreign workers into Singapore. You can also set up some of your businesses overseas and take advantage of the human resources of other countries that welcome your investment. The Internet also enables our companies to outsource some of their business operations overseas.

In this new world, I think countries will become less important and cities will become more important. There was a period in history, before the birth of nation-states, in which the Hanseatic League of cities drove European trade and economic growth, and were centres of civilisation. They joined together in a league in which they all practised free trade, enjoyed low taxes and the rule of law, and welcomed foreign talent. I want to argue that we now live in a new world of global cities. I want to argue that in this new global league of cities, Singapore will prosper. We will prosper not only because of our location, not only because we enjoy good governance, not only because we have educated and trained our human resource well, but also because of our multiculturalism. People used to think that homogeneous societies were advantaged, and heterogeneous societies were disadvantaged. I would argue that in the contemporary world, it is the homogeneous societies that are disadvantaged and heterogeneous societies advantaged.

I want to also say that as power shifts increasingly towards Asia, many of the leading cities of Asia will acquire global status. Singapore has very good credentials to bid to be the most globalised city of Asia. Why? Because, through an accident of history, we are at the confluence of the great civilisations of China, India and Southeast Asia. We are also at the crossroads of East and West. People of all different faith, colour and creed feel at home here.

I want to close by saying that merger with Malaysia is not an option we need to consider. Nizam, I do not know why you talked about re-merger with Malaysia. I was opposed to merger in 1963 and I am opposed to re-merger now. Singapore has grown and prospered as an independent country for nearly 45 years. Singapore will continue to thrive and prosper in the future. I am confident that Singapore will be one of the most attractive, competitive and liveable global cities of the world.

About the Contributors

Terence CHONG is a Fellow at the Institute of Southeast Asian Studies and Coordinator of its Regional Social and Cultural Studies Programme. He has a PhD in Sociology from the University of Warwick in the United Kingdom. His research interests include Singapore civil society, middle class and identity formations, the sociology of culture, Southeast Asian studies and globalisation theory. He has published in *Asian Studies Review*, *Journal of Contemporary Asia*, *Identities: Global Studies in Culture and Power*, *Social Identities*; and *Critical Asian Studies*.

GAN Su-lin has been the Director of the Centre for Culture and Communication at Republic Polytechnic (RP) since 2004, and concurrently served as the Founding Director of the School of Technology for the Arts from January 2005 to October 2007. Prior to RP, she was a tenured professor at Nanyang Technological University's School of Communication and Information, serving as Sub-Dean from 2001 to 2003. Su-lin gained her professional experience in journalism and public communications in Singapore, Brunei, Britain and the USA, the latter of which included a stint at CNN. Her academic training is in media psychology and her research focused on the palliative benefits of entertainment. Su-lin's dream is to live in a society of people with "Heads that understand, Hearts that empathise, Hands that freely give", and she is idiotically optimistic in her belief that while change may not happen in her lifetime, one still needs to start somewhere. Two hallmarks of Su-lin's approach to life are the measurement of personal wealth in terms of family ties, laughter, and giving, and in the romantically idealistic belief that giving should be done without expectation of returns.

Daniel PS GOH is Assistant Professor at the Department of Sociology, National University of Singapore. He specialises in comparative-historical sociology and cultural studies, but includes social ecology and comparative religion among his research interests. He has published in *Comparative Studies in Society and History*, the *International Journal of Cultural Studies*, *Actes de la Recherche en Sciences Sociale*, *Postcolonial Studies*,*Sociology Compass*, and has co-edited a volume on *Race and Multiculturalism in Malaysia and Singapore* (Routledge, 2009).

Annie KOH is Associate Professor of Finance and Dean of Office of Executive and Professional Education at the Singapore Management University. She is also concurrently the Associate Dean of the Lee Kong Chian School of Business and Academic Director of the International Trading Institute@SMU. She received her PhD in International Finance from New York University (Stern School of Business) in 1988 where she was a Fulbright scholar. Prior to joining academia, she was a treasury manager at DBS Bank. Annie is frequently sought after as a conference speaker, panel moderator and expert commentator. She also has extensive experience in consulting and executive teaching for regional and international banks, MNCs, government agencies, telecommunication companies, airlines, companies in the healthcare and hospitality sector, and not-for-profit organisations. Her articles have been published in *The Review of Future Markets*, *SIMEX Papers*, *Pulses*, and she authored IE Singapore's book on *Financing Internationalisation — Growth Strategies for Successful Companies*. Her current research interests are in Family Office and Family Business Research, REITS, Investor Behaviour, Alternative Investments, and Corporate Risk Management. She sits on several advisory boards and steering committees in the financial services and government sectors.

Tommy KOH is Ambassador-At-Large at the Ministry of Foreign Affairs, Chairman of the National Heritage Board and Special Adviser at the Institute of Policy Studies. He is also a Professor of Law at the National University of Singapore. He was Dean of the Law Faculty from 1971 to

1974 and Singapore's Permanent Representative to the United Nations in New York from 1968 to 1971 and from 1974 to 1984. He was Ambassador to the United States of America from 1984 to 1990, President of the Third UN Conference on the Law of the Sea where he chaired the Earth Summit, founding Chairman of the National Arts Council and the founding Executive Director of the Asia-Europe Foundation. He has served as the UN Secretary-General's Special Envoy to Russia, Estonia, Latvia and Lithuania, as well as Singapore's Chief Negotiator for the USA–Singapore Free Trade Agreement. He has chaired two dispute panels for the WTO.

Prof Koh received, in addition to his post-graduate qualifications from Harvard and Cambridge universities, honorary doctorates in law from Yale and Monash universities and various awards from Columbia, Stanford, Georgetown and Tufts universities.

LEE Hsien Loong was sworn in as Singapore's third Prime Minister in 2004. Mr Lee was first elected Member of Parliament (MP) in 1984 and has been re-elected in five consecutive elections. Mr Lee was appointed Minister of State in the Ministry of Trade and Industry (MTI) and the Ministry of Defence in 1984. He was confirmed as full Minister for Trade and Industry in 1987, and was concurrently Second Minister for Defence. In 1990, Mr Lee was appointed Deputy Prime Minister with responsibilities for economic and civil service matters. He also concurrently served as Chairman of the Monetary Authority of Singapore (MAS) from 1998 until 2004, and Minister for Finance from 2001 until 2007. As Prime Minister, Mr Lee has launched policies to build a competitive economy and an inclusive society. He has introduced new programmes to upgrade the education system, invest in R&D and infrastructure, and transform the city and living environment. Mr Lee's Government is also strengthening Singapore's social safety nets. Significant measures include the Workfare Incentive Scheme, which is a negative income tax to encourage and reward older, low-income workers, and Community Care (ComCare), an endowment fund to support a wide range of welfare and social programmes targeted at the poor. By tackling long-term issues such as the ageing population and the pressures of globalisation, Mr Lee seeks to gear up Singapore to seize the abundant opportunities in a vibrant Asia.

LEE Kwok Cheong has been the Chief Executive Officer of SIM Private Limited (SIM PL), an autonomous entity within Singapore Institute of Management (SIM Group), since August 2005. Prior to joining SIM, Kwok Cheong was the Group Chief Executive Officer of NCS Pte Ltd, a subsidiary of the SingTel Group, from 1995 to 2005. Under his leadership, NCS revenues grew from $138m to $668m. In 2001, he was a member of the Committee to Review Upgrading Opportunities at Degree Level, headed by Mr Peter Chen, then Senior Minister of State for Education and Trade and Industry. He was an Adjunct Associate Professor at NTU's Nanyang Business School from 1998 to 2002. Kwok Cheong currently sits on the board and chairs the Audit Committee of both Nanyang Polytechnic and the Institute of Technical Education. He was Chairman of the Policy Study Workgroup on Education and Human Capital Excellence (under REACH chaired by Dr Amy Khor) from October 2007 to September 2009, and is currently a Member of the Working Group for Schools under the National Integration Council, the "IT Working Group" as well as the "Best Home for Talents Work Group" of the Economic Strategies Committee, a Board Member of the Defence Science and Technology Agency (DSTA) and chair of the Casino Regulatory Authority's Technology Advisory Committee. A well-known figure in the IT industry, Kwok Cheong was Chairman of the Infocomm Manpower Council (IMC) from 2005 to 2008. He was the President of the Singapore Computer Society from 2004 to 2007 and was conferred Honorary Fellow in 2008. Born in Hong Kong, Kwok Cheong studied at the Massachusetts Institute of Technology (MIT) and the University of California at Berkeley. In 2001, he co-authored the book *Hi-Tech Hi-Touch Branding* with branding guru Dr Paul Temporal.

LEONG Ching is currently a PhD Candidate at the Lee Kuan Yew School of Public Policy, National University of Singapore. She studied in the National University of Singapore, where she graduated with an MA (Philosophy) in 1996. She joined *The Straits Times* thereafter and acquired an MBA in Information Technology (Surrey University) through distance learning. She later left to study under a Raffles Scholarship (now renamed Chevening Scholarship) for an MA (Journalism) at the University of London. On her return, she worked for a year in *The Straits Times* before joining Channel NewsAsia as Deputy Editor. She rejoined Singapore Press

Holdings on 1 July 2000. A year later, she became Assistant News Editor. In 2008, she left SPH to take up a scholarship for a doctoral program at the Lee Kuan Yew School of Public Policy. Leong Ching has been awarded the PBM and now sits on the council of the South West Community Development Council, headed by Mayor Amy Khor.

Aaron MANIAM is currently President of Mendaki Club, an organisation of young Singaporean Muslim professionals focused on capacity-building activities for Muslim students and professionals. He was appointed to the Board of Directors of Yayasan Mendaki in March 2009 and the Singapore Indian Development Association (SINDA) Executive Committee in April 2009. He chairs the Youth Sub-Committee at SINDA and is currently involved in the establishment of a Youth Club for Indian students and professionals. A member of the National Youth Council and an interfaith dialogue facilitator with Southeast CDC's "Explorations into Faiths" programme, Aaron read Philosophy, Politics and Economics (PPE) at Somerville College, Oxford University, on a Singapore Public Service Commission scholarship, graduating with double First Class Honours before pursuing an MA in International and Development Economics at Yale University. He was one of 25 Asia-Pacific young leaders named by the Asia Society as an "Asia 21 Fellow" in 2007.

Braema MATHIAPARANAM is currently the Chairperson/Coordinator of MARUAH (Singapore Working Group for an ASEAN Human Rights Mechanism) which is a human rights advocacy group. She is also the Regional President (Southeast Asia and Pacific Rim) for the International Council of Social Welfare, the chairperson of the CEDAW Committee at leading women's advocacy group, AWARE and Vice-President of Action for AIDS. From 2002 to 2007 she founded and led a migrant advocacy group, Transient Workers Count Too. Ms Braema continues to volunteer at such organisations while also working as a consultant researcher and trainer with local and international development-oriented agencies. She has worked as a teacher, as a journalist with *The Straits Times* and was the Gender Studies Programme Coordinator and Visiting Research Fellow at the Institute of Southeast Asian Studies. She was also a two-term Nominated Member of Parliament.

NIZAM Idris is Executive Director and Head of Asia Emerging Markets Strategy at UBS AG. He is responsible for Asia macroeconomic research and for formulating trade ideas and short to medium-term forecasts for all emerging Asia currencies and rates outlook for both external and internal clients. Nizam publishes the occasional strategy highlights and research comments on Asian economies to help maintain clients' understanding of the latest thematic issues influencing Asian markets and economies. Before joining UBS in March 2006, he worked as an economist at IDEAglobal for 11 years, where he last held the position of Deputy Chief Economist for Asia. His work at IDEAglobal spanned both economics research and currency strategy. He holds a Master's degree in Economics and Econometrics from the University of Manchester and a BSc in Economics from the National University of Singapore. Nizam also served as a member of the Board of Directors at the Energy Market Authority and a member of the Private Education Appeals Board at the Ministry of Education. He was also a member of the Resource Panels at the Government Parliamentary Committees for Trade and Industry and Finance.

ONG Keng Yong is Director of the Institute of Policy Studies in the Lee Kuan Yew School of Public Policy at the National University of Singapore. He is concurrently Ambassador-At-Large in the Singapore Ministry of Foreign Affairs and Singapore's Non-Resident Ambassador to Iran. He was Secretary-General of ASEAN (Association of Southeast Asian Nations) from January 2003 to January 2008. His diplomatic postings took him to Saudi Arabia, Malaysia and the USA. He was Singapore's Ambassador to India and Nepal from 1996–1998. He was appointed Press Secretary to the Prime Minister of Singapore and concurrently held senior positions in the Ministry of Information, Communications and the Arts, and the People's Association in Singapore from 1998–2002. He is a graduate of the University of Singapore and Georgetown University (Washington DC, USA).

PEK Siok Lian is Executive Producer at Journey Pictures and an award-winning journalist and documentary filmmaker with a reputation for tackling sensitive, difficult topics with an unflinching yet compassionate eye. Her debut film for the Discovery Channel, *Sayonara Changi* gave the world an unprecedented look inside Singapore's former Changi Prison, one of Asia's most notorious jails during World War Two and the Guantanamo of its time. Her most recent film *Mad About English* tracked China's obsession with the English language to much acclaim, becoming the highest-grossing Singaporean documentary in local cinema history. Her documentary work can be found on CBC, Discovery Channel, History Channel, NHK, Phoenix TV, Al-Jazeera English, etc. Prior to programme-making, Siok Lian was the first Singaporean Anchor/Correspondent hired by CNN International, winning the Best Current Affairs Presenter award at the 6th Asia TV Awards. Prior to CNN, she was the bureau head for TV at Bloomberg Financial News. She began her broadcast career at the Television Corporation of Singapore, creating the first daily business bulletin as the network's youngest Business Editor. Siok Lian won a Television Corporation of Singapore scholarship to read English at the National University of Singapore where she graduated with B.A. Honours. She also holds a Master's in Theatre Arts from Goldsmiths College, University of London. She currently serves as a board member with one of Singapore's foremost theatre companies Action Theatre, having previously served as an artistic associate with the NUS Centre for the Arts.

TAN Tarn How is a Senior Research Fellow at the Institute of Policy Studies. His research areas are in arts and cultural policy and media and Internet policy. He has written on the development of the arts in Singapore, in particular, fostering partnerships between the people, private and public sectors, on the creative industries in Singapore, China and Korea, on the history of cultural policy in Singapore, on censorship, and on the management of media in Singapore. He has also carried out research on the impact of the Internet and new technology on society, the regulation of the Internet, the role of new media in the 2008 Malaysian election and the 2006 Singapore election, and the impact of new media on old media. He was a journalist for nearly one and half decades before joining IPS. He has also been a teacher and television scriptwriter and is an award-winning playwright. He graduated from Cambridge University.

Paulin TAY STRAUGHAN is Associate Professor at the Sociology Department at the National University of Singapore. She is also Vice-Dean of the Faculty of Arts and Social Sciences. She received her PhD from the University of Virginia, and completed her undergraduate degree at NUS. Her current research focus is on preventive health behaviour, and community reaction to emerging infectious diseases. She also researches on family issues, and has recently published two books in this area: *Marriage Dissolution in Singapore* (Brill) and *Ultra-low Fertility in Pacific Asia* (Routledge). She is married to Dr Robert Straughan and they have two teenage sons.

Henry Wai-chung YEUNG, PhD, is Professor of Economic Geography at the Department of Geography, National University of Singapore. He was a recipient of many research awards, including Outstanding Researcher Award from National University of Singapore, the Commonwealth Fellowship, the Fulbright Foreign Research Award, and the Rockefeller Foundation's Team Residency in Bellagio. His research interests cover broadly theories and the geography of transnational corporations, Asian firms and their overseas operations and Chinese business networks in the Asia-Pacific region. Professor Yeung is the author of four books and editor or co-editor of another five books. He has over 80 research papers published or forthcoming in internationally refereed journals and 38 chapters in books. He is Editor of *Environment and Planning A, Economic Geography*, and *Review of International Political Economy*, Asia-Pacific Editor of *Global Networks*, Contributing Editor of *International Journal of Urban and Regional Research*, and Business Manager of *Singapore Journal of Tropical Geography*. He sits on the editorial boards of 11 other international journals in the fields of human geography, management, urban studies, area studies, and general social science.